In His Image

In His Image

A Biblical Introduction to Social Ethics

Dr Stephen McQuoid

Wilberforce Publications
London

Published in Great Britain in 2020 by
Wilberforce Publications Limited
70 Wimpole Street, London W1G 8AX

Wilberforce Publications Limited is a wholly owned subsidiary of Christian Concern.

ISBN 978-1-9995842-9-0

British Library Cataloguing Data
A catalogue record for this book is available from the British Library.

Printed in Great Britain by Imprint Digital, Exeter
and worldwide

Contents

Acclaim for Stephen McQuoid's books

The Quest for True Tolerance, Day One (2007)

McQuoid analyses, with devastating clarity, the shallow tolerance which passes as broadmindedness, and exposes its intolerant superficiality. He argues that true tolerance and respect for others, in Christian understanding, is based on both truth and love. The Quest for True Tolerance is a much needed and long-overdue contribution to a critically important debate. Its author is to be congratulated for giving us such a succinct and insightful treatment of a difficult and confusing subject.

Dr Alistair Noble, Director, The Centre for Intelligent Design and former Education Officer, CARE Scotland

The Beginner's Guide to Expository Preaching, Christian Focus (2002)

Stephen McQuoid writes out of the conviction that "the church urgently needs a new generation of preachers". A well-crafted manual on preaching, it is surprisingly comprehensive for its size, and is marked by practicality and realism. Both emerging and established preachers cannot fail to profit from it.

The late **Derek Prime**, Pastor of Charlotte Chapel in Edinburgh and President of FIEC

Stephen McQuoid shares his own preaching experience to great effect as he firmly roots the importance of preaching biblically and historically and practically. We need preachers who will communicate to the highest standard – and this book will help.

McQuoid will succeed in making preachers think hard about the passion, preparation, style and development of their preaching gift. I trust it will be a blessing and a challenge to them – it certainly was for me.

Derek Lamont, Senior Minister of St Columba's Free Church of Scotland in Edinburgh

The Beginner's Guide to Expository Preaching, Christian Focus (2002)

Yet another book on preaching? Yes! For those who preach can never receive enough instruction, stimulation and encouragement for their work. And few things are more stimulating to preachers than listening to or reading what a fellow preacher has to say on this subject. Stephen McQuoid's readily digestible and stimulating new book will help seasoned preachers and enable them to give themselves a good check-up. Beginners will benefit from the straightforward and sensible counsel he gives. And some who never preach may be helped to pray for and encourage those who do. So, I for one am grateful for the labour of love this little manual represents and warmly welcome it.

Sinclair B. Ferguson, Chancellor's Professor of Systematic Theology, Reformed Theological Seminary, USA and formerly Minister at St. George's Tron Church, Glasgow

A New Kind of Living, Christian Focus (1998)

Stephen McQuoid's book is geared to helping new Christians find their feet as they begin to grow in their newfound faith. It is straightforward, honest and realistic as it works through what it means to know and follow Jesus Christ. Rich in practical help and thoroughly grounded in Scripture, this book can help 'old hands' get refocused as well as providing building blocks for new Christians. It will prove to be an enormously helpful resource for those running nurture groups.

Andy Bathgate, former Chief Executive, Scripture Union Scotland

FOREWORD

Jesus said: "If you love me, you will obey my commandments" (John 14:15). He also said that the most important commandments are to love God, and to love your neighbour as yourself (Matt. 22:38-39). This love of neighbour includes everyone we come into contact with, and ultimately mandates us to seek God's best for the good of society.

At the root of the concern that Christians have to seek the best for all people is the understanding that we are all made in God's image. Human life is sacred. From conception to natural death, every person should be cared for and respected. Alongside this is the family as the bedrock of society – with all that this means for our relationships and sexual ethics.

As one of the founders of Christian Concern, my passion is to see this nation turning back to its Christian roots. We have sadly abandoned God's laws in so many ways. What we need now is a moral revolution to recover God's rules for living.

It is my prayer that this book will contribute to such a moral revolution. It is a book that imparts understanding in a clear and accessible manner. In a world of conflicting voices, the voice of the church needs clarity and compassion. This book helps to sharpen that voice with a solid biblical grounding.

As Christians living in this generation, part of our call is to be a voice for the voiceless, and to challenge the culture when it stands against God and His ways. Christians need to be equipped to be ambassadors for Christ as we witness for Him. This book will equip you to speak prophetically to this generation – to defend the unborn, the sick, the elderly, and to defend marriage and biblical sexual ethics.

My prayer as you read this book is that God will stir your heart to be one of His ambassadors. God wants to equip you to speak out with boldness for the truth. Many people are captivated by lies. It is the truth that will set people free. Read it, digest it, and then tell it. A new generation of bold Christians speaking with clarity and conviction can change the culture.

Ade Omooba MBE
Co-founder, Christian Concern

PREFACE

This is a book that I have been wanting to write for quite some time. Like many Christians, I have had a significant concern about moral decline in much of the Western world, including the United Kingdom. As an evangelist I pray for my neighbours and unchurched friends and try to share with them the good news about Jesus. Ultimately, the gospel is the only thing that will bring transformation and return our culture to its Judaeo-Christian roots. That said, while we wait and pray for revival, I passionately believe that Christians need to speak out about what is going wrong in our culture, while at the same time speaking for truth.

At the heart of the ethical war that rages in our society today are issues of human identity and sexuality. Nowhere is the fallenness of humanity more evident than with these issues. Abortion is the silent genocide that is claiming millions of innocent lives all over the world. There is an assault on marriage, an institution given by God to bring stability and cohesion to the family, which in turn supports society as a whole. Then there is the issue of gender – the distinctive and dignified identity that God has given each one of us so that we can be men and women made in the image of God. Each of these areas is an ethical battleground.

There are many people I would like to thank for their assistance during this project. Firstly, I would like to thank Christian Concern and their publishing wing Wilberforce Publications. This is not just because they have published this book, but because they are a group of committed believers who want to contend for truth in our culture and their courageous efforts should be applauded. I am particularly grateful to John Scriven whose wise advice helped to shape this book at its earliest stages.

There are also two doctors whose advice and input were invaluable, especially in dealing with the medical aspects of this book: Dr Linda McKerlie, a GP, and Dr Paul Coulter, doctor, theologian and

Christian leader. Both of them gave helpful advice, wise counsel and encouragement and helped me to understand the complexities involved. A special thanks goes to Stephen Shaw QC, brilliant barrister and Bible teacher who read the manuscript and greatly assisted my thinking processes. He did so with characteristic graciousness, and I am thankful for his ability to think hard yet speak gently about the flaws of my argument. Sam Webster of the Christian Institute put my mind at rest by checking that I did not cross any lines as I made my case. I have been indebted to him before and am thankful for the work that he does.

Thanks also to Anne Grover of Tilsley College. She willingly proofread the manuscript, highlighting its many typos, inaccuracies and confusing sections, thus saving my blushes. Her patience was evidenced by a willingness to go through the manuscript twice with a fine-tooth comb, and the end result is all the better for it. I owe all the above a great debt and I must state that opinions expressed are mine and not necessarily theirs, as are any errors in the text.

A final thanks must go to my wife Debbie whose passion for justice, truth and Christian values has always been an inspiration to me. It is easy to stand up and be counted in a fallen world when married to someone who shares my desire for God's will being done on earth as it is in heaven.

Christians should never be judgmental. We all have feet of clay and we must walk humbly in this life. However, we do need to be salt and light and to stand up for Christian truth. This book is my attempt to do just that in the context of a culture that is turning its back on the Creator's instructions, which bring health and wholeness.

INTRODUCTION

The issues addressed in this book depend upon fundamental truths revealed by God in Scripture. The Bible is therefore the essential starting point in Part 1 (chapters 1 and 2). Part 2 builds upon that foundation, and in chapters 3 and 4 there is discussion of how God has provided for the moral dimensions of human life, focusing on particular ethical issues. Chapters 5, 6 and 7 deal with some of the most significant ethical issues that we face as a society today. In Part 3, the role of the church is examined – both the visible institution and the 'invisible' church of all faithful believers in Jesus Christ.

In such a short volume, this review of some of the challenges to biblical ethics and a Christian response cannot be comprehensive; some further related points mentioned below may be helpful to readers wishing to explore further.

First, there is the use of the word 'love'. I deliberately opt for the distinctively Christian usage of the word and concept of 'love'. This is a translation of the Greek term 'agape', which means unselfish caring (including actions) for others. This is the kind of love that God has for all of us and was perfectly exemplified by Jesus in His relationships with others. The usual English word 'love', on the other hand, is commonly taken to refer to a number of things including, for example, 'attraction' of one kind or another (both romantic and sexual). The 'agape' love is considered in chapter 9, but this is a distinction which needs to be borne in mind throughout. It is simply not the same from a qualitative point of view, as a mere romantic or sexual attraction which may lack the self-giving and unselfish component. It is this true agape love that Christians are to demonstrate as they care for people in society.

There is also a presupposition of immutability of sexual orientation in what is often called 'progressive' thought. This presumption actually runs counter to empirical evidence, yet it usually passes unchallenged, for philosophical reasons. Often this is because those who hold to this presupposition wish to delegitimate any form of reparative therapy, again for philosophical rather than purely scientific reasons.

In all of this debate there is an important distinction which needs to be made between thoughts and temptations and sinful acts. There can also be a rejection of the notion of 'sin', even among people who claim to be Christians. Sin is real and the Bible is also realistic about our fallen human nature. Biblical morality is clearly articulated in Scripture and we are also told that resisting temptation is good. Indeed, it is an essential element in discipleship, and the Holy Spirit aids Christian believers whose desire is to be holy. Holiness is, of course, much more than simply resisting temptation, but this is nevertheless a vital part of the spiritual battle for every Christian believer and one that we should not shrink from.

Part 1

Theology: Understanding the Biblical Foundations

Chapter 1

Image Bearers

The world is a truly wonderful place, full of beauty and colour. Few could be so hard-hearted as to be unappreciative of the myriad plants and animals that fill Planet Earth with life. All of this is evidence of a grand designer who created all this beauty and wonder and blended it together to form the magnificent entity that we often refer to as 'nature'. As the Apostle Paul declared in his famous letter to the Romans, 'God's invisible qualities – his eternal power and divine nature – have been clearly seen, being understood from what has been made' (Rom. 1:20).

However, much as we might admire the beauty of the natural world, there is one part of the created order that seems more glorious and precious than all the rest and that is the human race. Such a statement could be met with the accusation of 'speciesism' by those who refuse to see humankind as something more than advanced animals. Highly developed and intelligent, yes, but just animals nonetheless.

The Bible tells a very different story, because it describes humans as being the very pinnacle of creation, the highest beings a Creator God decided to make, with qualities that only God has. It is this perspective that gives humans their unique place in a Judaeo-Christian worldview and to which I shall turn shortly. However, before we explore this, it would be useful to reflect upon the uniqueness of humankind in a world of such beauty and wonder. What is the practical evidence for this?

Intelligence

The first is the quality we commonly refer to as intelligence. Nature lovers might quickly note that we see intelligence in the animal kingdom in such creatures as dolphins, elephants and birds. Indeed, some animals such as chimpanzees even demonstrate problem-solving intelligence.

It is surely arrogance, it is said, to boast about the superior intelligence of humans.

However, any comparison between human and animal intelligence falls down, not because the two are so similar, but rather because the two are so far apart from each other. Indeed, it is not even meaningful to make a comparison between human intelligence and that of even the most intelligent animals, because human intelligence is so obviously superior. Reflect, for example, on human ability in mathematics. Many of the calculations we make are abstract ideas because the numbers we use do not represent any physical or tangible objects. Even something as simple as understanding and reciting the times tables is well beyond the abilities of any animal. Then there are the human advances in computing, engineering and medicine and our ability to think critically and reason philosophically. All of these elevate humans to a totally different level of intellectual experience from that of animals.

Self-awareness

Secondly, we can reflect upon the self-awareness that is a significant motivation for humans. It is part of being human to be concerned about how we look, and this sense is so finely tuned that it affects our self-esteem. If we have 'let ourselves go' and generally look dishevelled, a glance in the mirror might depress us. Likewise, if we change our appearance or purchase some new clothes that flatter us, the opposite emotion occurs in front of that same mirror.

Some might argue that animals also preen themselves when looking for a mate and creatures like the peacock fan out their plumage as they show off their attributes. While that is true, it is an instinctive act of seduction or perhaps a sign of authority, establishing a 'pecking order'. That seems a long way off from the kind of self-awareness that produces global industries in clothing, cosmetics, perfumes and fashion. Moreover, humans need to feel good about themselves, whether or not it gives them power or partners. The need to be aware of oneself and to present oneself appropriately is a profound, deep-rooted, as well as a highly sophisticated psychological need, which is distinctly human.

Creativity

We next think of the quality of creativity. This too is seen in lavish quantities in the human world. Again, some might argue that animals can manifest creativity in what they do. Anyone who has seen the nest of a village weaver bird, or who has glanced inside a honeycomb or even an anthill, cannot fail to be impressed with what these animals can do. However, it is doubtful whether this can be seen as creativity, rather than just an instinctive ability to build a particular thing in a specific way. After all, ants and birds are not known to construct radically new styles of nest, or bees to add different nuances to their honeycomb. So clearly there are limitations to what animals can create, if indeed they do create. However, when we look at the extent and variety of human creativity, it clearly separates us from the animal kingdom and makes us unique.

Think for a moment of the work of the Dutch Masters or perhaps the French Impressionists. Consider the genius of Leonardo da Vinci, who painted the exotic Mona Lisa so delicately that people have long debated whether she is smiling or not. Then look at the bizarre works of Salvador Dali such as The Persistence of Memory, or The Lugubrious Game or the magisterial Christ of Saint John of the Cross. Compare all of these to The Scream by Edvard Munch or the modern art of Damien Hirst and you realise the vast creativity of which humans are capable. This is without even thinking of the music we have created – the symphonies and sacred works of Bach, Beethoven or Mozart, the jazz trumpeting of Miles Davis, or the influential sounds of Bob Dylan. Moving from the arts to engineering, we wonder at the marvels of St Peter's Basilica in Rome, the Sydney Opera House, the Taj Mahal, the Alhambra and the Burj Khalifa. It is not hard to see in all of this the uniqueness of human creativity as it reinvents itself again and again. Nothing in the animal kingdom can compare with it.

Morality, nobility, altruism and spirituality

Beyond these qualities there are those of nobility, altruism, morality and spirituality. These are transcendent qualities that again distinguish humanity from the rest of creation. Our sense of morality is something innate. We just know that some things are wrong, and we react strongly to them. This sense of wrong is fairly consistent across cultures and people groups. You could travel to different parts of the world and meet diverse peoples, all of whom would regard the abuse of children, or rape, or premeditated murder as wrong. Of course, these may well happen in all countries because we often, as human beings, fail to live up to our own standards of morality. However, such actions are nonetheless condemned and discouraged, and their punishment is a hallmark of a civilised society.

That sense of morality expresses itself in the valuing of human life. We see human life as being sacred and to be protected. If we observe a lion on the Serengeti attacking and devouring an antelope, we assume that this is a normal part of nature. On the other hand, if we witness one human being bludgeoned to death by another, we call it murder and demand justice. Such is the elevated way in which we prize human life.

Something more of the specialness of humanity can be seen in the altruistic behaviour to which we can aspire. During the First and Second World Wars many young men and women voluntarily enlisted knowing that their lives could come to a premature and violent end. They did so to protect both their loved ones, and also their fellow citizens, most of whom they did not know and would never meet. The sense of nobility lies so deep that people are willing to make the ultimate sacrifice for abstract ideas such as freedom, democracy and liberty.

Then there is the human capacity for spirituality. As human beings, we seem instinctively drawn to see beyond ourselves and to desire a relationship with the divine. Worshipping communities can be found in every corner of the world; it is as if we have an inbuilt inclination to look to something or someone greater than ourselves. That sense of reverence, an inclination to the spiritual, is again something that is unique to humanity, distinguishing us from the rest of creation.

Creation

What we appear to sense about the nature of humanity, the Bible confirms, as it tells the story of creation. During the first five days of the creation story, God spoke matter into existence and then life in its various forms. At the end of each day God reflected on what He had created, and on each occasion declared that it was good (Gen. 1:10). However, on the sixth day God came to His greatest act of creation, that of human beings. Having prepared a world for them to inhabit, God then made them. In doing so He declared that it was very good (Gen. 1:31). Humans were the pinnacle of God's creation, the most wonderful, precious and important thing that God made. This is why we are special – because God made us to be so.

Image of God

Something else of supreme significance should be noted from the story of creation. At each point in the creation story God was making a universe from His own magnificent imagination. However, when He created humans, the blueprint was Himself. Humans are made in the very image of God and it is this that makes us unique and of inherent value (Gen. 1:26-27). It is here that we begin to unpack the importance of humanity and also to lay a foundation for our ethics. Any understanding of our place in the universe must begin with an understanding of creation and our relationship with God.

Before we get there, we need to define what we mean by being made 'in the image of God'. It is clearly a significant issue because only humans were made in this way. The image of God in man is expressly stated in Genesis 1:26 where we are told God said, 'Let us make man in our image, after our likeness'. Put simply, being made in the image of God means that man is, in some sense, like God and represents God in the world.[1] The Hebrew words for image (*tselem*) and for likeness (*demut*) refer to something that is similar to another thing, but not identical. They can also be used to denote something that represents something else. In the context of man being made in God's image, man is made like God and can represent Him or mediate His will and purposes.

Throughout church history, theologians have endeavoured to precisely locate one of more definite characteristics that are the connection point or similarity between man and God. Some have seen it as human intelligence or our capacity for morality, or even our original moral purity. However, there is no need to limit the identification to just one quality. As we have already noted, human beings are special and unique in all of creation. We can readily see that humans are, in so many ways, superior to anything within the animal kingdom. This supremacy in all its beauty and glory is what distinguishes us from the animals, and this is because God, who is supreme over all, has made us like Himself. Obviously, we cannot compare ourselves to the greatness and majesty of God. We are creatures and He is Creator, but elements of human uniqueness reflect something of the character and nature of God.

Given that we are made in God's image, humans have a value and a worth that is greater than that of any other creature. The created world was 'good'; we as humans are 'very good'. This value which God places on us is innate and cannot be removed. It therefore becomes a fixed reference point for ethics. The value of human life, which is predicated on us being made in God's image, informs us as to how all human beings are to be treated.

Male and Female

Before we move on, there is something else that we need to note which is of great significance to ethics. Not only does Genesis tell us that we are made in God's image, but the very next verse (Gen. 1:27) states that, 'In the image of God he created them; male and female he created them'. This expression tells us two very significant things about the image of God. First, it tells us that both men and women are bearers of the image of God and they possess it equally. Men and women, in both masculinity and femininity, are carriers of the image of God and are representatives of God.

Secondly, we can go further; Genesis 1 is a description of the perfect world that God created. This is the world as it ought to be. Consequently, not only do both men and women bear the image of God, but the two genders which God intended and therefore created are expressed here. There is much contemporary debate about the fluidity of gender, and this will be discussed later. However, the fixed categories of male and female are the only ones expressed in the creation narrative.

Perfect Fit

There is still more for us to look at in the creation story. When we get to Genesis 2, we have a different and fuller explanation of creation. The narrative describes God's thinking in the creation of human beings. The passage records the creation of the man (Adam). Then a penetrating statement is made by God in verse 18 when He declares that 'it is not good for man to be alone. I will make a suitable helper for him'. This is a verse of immense significance because God presents His template for the kind of relationship that will sustain the human race. He is about to create a partner for Adam and this partner will be 'suitable', the perfect fit for Adam in God's plan for the world.

Complementarity is very important in the jigsaw puzzle of life. Only a piece that is a perfect fit will meet the requirements that God intended. There is a diversion in the narrative in verses 19 and 20 as God creates all manner of wildlife, which Adam duly names. As an image bearer, he has responsibility under God for all of creation. However, verse 20 ends with a poignant statement that 'for Adam no suitable helper was found'. This is not just theology; it is brilliant prose. The tension is being built up in the passage to make a supremely important point. The creation of all kinds of animals, each with their partner, highlighted the need for a partner for Adam, but it had to be the right one, someone whom God deemed suitable.

Adam is put into a deep sleep (v. 21) and then God takes a rib from him with which He will create Eve. This, of course, is poetry. But in the dramatic imagery of this poetry there is a fundamental truth. The suitable partner for Adam is Eve. Female is the perfect balance and companion to male. If chapter 1 tells us that the perfect categorisation is the binary categories of male and female, chapter 2 tells us that the perfect life partner for the man is a woman. If the power of this point is missed by the reader, verse 24 amplifies it by providing a rationale for why female is the perfect complement to male. The two become 'one flesh'. Clearly, among other things, this expression implies a sexual union when the perfect fit is amply demonstrated by the capacity for procreation (Gen. 1:28). It should be recognised that the act of procreation is only possible when male and female come together, and this is all by God's design.

Social

As well as creating us sexual beings, God has made us social beings. Society is part of the created order. As humanity we live together, look after the earth (Gen. 1:28) and develop our relationships and culture. Society and culture are part of God's design; He made us social beings so that we could relate to one another. He instilled in us a sense of morality so that we could live respectfully with one another and mirror in human relationships the relationship we have with God. Work was also part of this masterplan. Mankind was to steward the world and cultivate it (Gen. 1:26), so as to make it productive. By doing so, a cohesive society could be built that would provide a livelihood and protection for human beings.

This then was God's plan in creation: a world in which human beings could thrive, live in community and be productive. This is much more than just a description of how God created the physical world and the people who occupy it. The creation narratives point to a world as it ought to be, and one that would contribute to human flourishing. Today, in the name of freedom, we are trying to turn on its head the plan that God designed. As humans do this, they are not only rebelling against the Creator, they are also tampering with the original plan for human flourishing. This is inevitably an act of self-harm.

Note

[1] Wayne Grudem, *Systematic Theology*, p. 442.

Chapter 2

Paradise Lost: The Fall and its Consequences

In chapter 1 we looked at the Genesis creation narratives which give us a template for the world that God intended. The world we now inhabit is a far cry from the paradise that the first two chapters of Genesis describe. The reason for the change is an event, described in Genesis 3, that we refer to as 'the Fall'. It is here that the paradise that God had intended was ruined as a result of our human desire for autonomy.

Genesis 3 is a passage full of irony, because humanity sought betterment by becoming independent from the Creator. However, like any designed thing, when we ignore the Maker's instructions it can only end in tears. The consequences of the events that took place were not only cataclysmic at the time, but they affect humanity to this day. It was here that the relationship between creature and Creator was broken; the impact on humanity was immense.

Before dealing with the passage we need to remind ourselves of some of the things that we learnt from the previous chapters. First, God made a world that was perfect and allowed for human flourishing. It was a place where He and humanity could be in harmony and where humans could also live successfully together, utilising all that God had provided for their needs. This paradise, however, was dependent on keeping to the design instructions.

Secondly, mankind was created in the image of God as morally free beings with the ability to make authentic choices and to enjoy the benefits or suffer the consequences of whatever choices were made.

What we do not learn from the creation narratives but do learn from other passages of Scripture is that, prior to these events, an angelic rebellion occurred that resulted in Satan and his minions being cast out of heaven, and becoming the implacable enemies of God. The 'sin' mentioned in chapter 3 was therefore not the first sin to be committed, but it was the first human sin. It was encouraged by Satan, who is determined to oppose everything God does.

Chapter 3 clearly contains poetry, but what cannot be doubted is that it describes, in whatever form, a conscious rebellion against the Designer's plans, and one that had catastrophic consequences. I take the position that this chapter describes a real historical event, not least because the New Testament talks of the Fall in a very tangible way. I will therefore unpack it as such.

The chapter begins (v. 1) with the writer describing the serpent as being, 'more crafty than any of the beasts of the field'. The Devil, in the form of a serpent, comes to Adam and Eve with the purpose of encouraging a rebellion against the Creator and His plans. He has a clear plan of action. Initially he begins to undermine the Creator by raising questions about what God has said. He challenged Eve in verse 1 with the words 'did God actually say?' and then deliberately misquoted God's words. This was a clever tactic, because if he had begun by openly contradicting God and His word, Eve might have been shocked and become defensive. Instead, he raised doubts and sowed confusion, which began to develop scepticism in Eve's mind.

There is an important matter to note here. The destruction of any worldview often begins with a subtle undermining and a fraying at the edges. Eve foolishly engaged in conversation with the serpent even though she knew the authority of God was being questioned. She reiterated the message God had given her and Adam, namely that the whole garden had been granted to them with the exception of the one tree in the centre of the garden, which was off limits – anyone who ate its fruit would be punished with death.

The serpent's response is interesting. Having already questioned the validity of God's word, he began to deny openly God's word by stating in verse 4, 'You will not surely die'. In other words: God is a liar, He is not telling the truth, you are naïve to believe God, this is an assault on your autonomy.

Contemporary Questioning of Truth

It is not hard to see modern cultural parallels in all of this. The Judaeo-Christian worldview has been under siege in European culture at least since the Enlightenment. There have been concerted attempts in academic circles to 'demythologise' Scripture, which would rob it of its authority and power. More broadly, many forces within our culture have tried to marginalise and privatise faith, so as to make it a peripheral aspect of contemporary life, with no presence or power in national cultural life. People are allowed to worship God and believe His word provided they do not say that Scripture has something to say to society as a whole. This battle for the hearts and minds of the nation is spiritual as well as philosophical.

Another point must be noted. The Devil did not just attack God's word, he also questioned the very idea that there might be consequences for rebellion: that is, he questioned the concept of judgment. The effectiveness of this can be seen today by the fact that our culture regards any notion of divine judgment as an anathema. The god modern culture accepts is a deity who smiles at us while turning a blind eye to all of our wrongdoing. The idea that God might play the role of moral overseer is one which is strongly rejected today even though, as Dostoyevsky warned, without the benefit of this safeguard, anything can be considered permissible.

Something else emerges in this passage. The serpent declared to Eve that, 'God knows that if you do eat you will be like God, knowing good and evil' (v. 5). His claim was that humans should be able to act autonomously and decide for themselves how they should behave and what their moral parameters should be. Rather than relying on God to be the moral law giver, they should take this role on themselves, thus turning morality into a subjective human exercise. This, the serpent said, was something God knew and feared, because morally autonomous human beings would consequently be beyond His control.

It is not hard to see how the disintegration of the Judaeo-Christian worldview in contemporary society has led to a rapid change in ethics. This is the natural consequence of rejecting God's objective moral standards. It is played out in the central feature of this story (v. 6). Eve looked at the fruit, saw that it 'looked delicious' and wanted some.

Knowing what God had said, she decided for herself what she should do. The irony is that her freedom to make a moral choice and to decide for herself was granted to her by God in the first place, as part of her being made in the image of God.

Free Will, Responsibility and Consequence

That same moral free will carries with it a huge responsibility. As humans we are free to choose, but are also responsible for the consequences of our choices. This is why God is not culpable for the harm we humans suffer as a result of our own choices. The privilege of true humanity demands the living of life with responsibility, knowing that our actions carry consequences.

Having wilfully taken the fruit, Eve 'gave it to Adam', who joined her in this defiance of God's law. The impact on them was immediate and dramatic, namely they 'realised their nakedness' (v. 7). This was the first time that humans felt a sense of shame and guilt. They hid from God because Paradise had been lost and they were responsible. An important lesson here is that true paradise is not giving expression to our own moral impulses, but recognising that there are moral laws beyond ourselves that are given to enhance our lives. To disobey them is profoundly damaging to ourselves.

Other ramifications followed swiftly. First, there was the blame game (vv. 12-13), as no one wanted to take responsibility for what had happened. It was someone else's fault! Then judgment was passed on the serpent (vv. 14-15), before finally being passed on humanity (vv. 16-19). We need to be careful how we interpret these verses. The lesson here is not limited to the narrow issue of the pain of childbirth as evidence of the Fall; it is much broader than this. In Paradise there was no human suffering, because God was sovereign and created an environment where humanity could be protected from the pain of suffering. In the new fallen world things were different. Humans had rejected God's rule, preferring freedom from it, and consequently, suffering became part of the life they had now chosen. This suffering includes natural causes, man's inhumanity to man, disease and death. All of these things happened when God, the giver and sustainer of life, was kept at arm's length and His rule rejected. They are just some examples of a world gone wrong, but the list could prove endless.

Finally, Adam and Eve were 'banished from the garden' (vv. 22-24). God would not continue to have an intimate and trusting relationship with people who did not recognise His lordship. The Fall was human rebellion against God and a striving for autonomy. It began with the questioning, and then rejection, of God's word, which led to the defining of morality without reference to God.

Given the Fall with all of its consequences, a response was needed if the damage was to be limited. First, there was the need for a culturally transcendent law. Then, there was the need for personal transformation.

Part 2

Contemporary: Understanding Ethical Challenges

Chapter 3

The Need for Moral Foundations

Most people believe in the importance of morality, whether or not they are religiously inclined. There would be a widescale recognition that murder, child abuse and common injustices are wrong. The vast majority of people would insist that the world would be a better place if these values, which most people seem to hold to, were universal and enforceable. The challenge arises, however, when we widen out the moral issues and when we begin a discussion about the basis of ethics. This is because the consensus breaks down on both specific issues and the foundations of our morality and a clear division emerges, principally between theists and secularists.

Theists believe that God defines what is right and wrong, but understandably, most people who claim no religious affiliation cannot accept this. Theists, and in particular Christians, have views on issues such as abortion, gender fluidity and same-sex marriage that are not shared by most people in society, particularly non-religious people. This creates a tension that deserves to be explored. Why do Christians hold to the views they do, and why would they assume that their ethical standards can inform wider society?

We begin by thinking more broadly about how our wider culture arrives at some of its ethical standards. How does our society do ethics? The answer to this is not simple because, as a society, we have developed a number of different ethical models to assist us in navigating life. I will mention just a few.

Some choose to live by what could best be termed a principle ethic, that is, they try to live according to some prescribed set of standards that have been codified and preserved. Christians use this model because they base their ethical standards on the Bible, which they believe to be the revealed will of God. The same would apply to Muslims and to some other religions; their holy books reveal the standards which they are to live by. Even people with no religious inclination might favour a principle ethic. The principles they follow may have evolved gradually within broader culture, or they may simply subscribe to a set of values which they find appealing or useful.

Others choose consequential ethics, that is: they decide on the rightness or wrongness of an action depending on the outcome of that action.[2] For example, a person may argue that lying is wrong because it breaks down trust and therefore damages relationships. That same person might also exaggerate their tax expenses, which is also lying, but could justify this action on the basis that no one is specifically being harmed. It is still lying, but not morally wrong (apparently) because there are no damaging consequences. Likewise, telling a lie to protect someone or to spare their feelings would be morally acceptable because of the benefit to the person being protected.

Some might practise a kind of virtue ethic. In this model, an action carried out by someone who is considered to be a good person becomes a good action by virtue of the individual doing the action. In short, if they do it and they are good, the action must be good. This model gives great moral power to people like the late Nelson Mandela or the Pope or even someone like Greta Thunberg. Goodness is measured in relation to the person, rather than the action standing on its own merits.

Still others utilise contextual ethics. Here what makes an action right or wrong is the wider context. In China the widespread termination of unborn children was justified on the basis of population control. It was deemed acceptable because of the context and the implication for the country as a whole. Likewise, there is great moral pressure exerted today not to eat red meat or to use plastic carrier bags because of their environmental impact. An action is justified not on its own basis, but on the impact that it has on the wider world.

This list of ethical systems is far from exhaustive and they are not mutually exclusive, as people may use several models concurrently in their ethical decision-making. This can often make ethical decisions complex and leave us with a feeling of uncertainty as to whether we have made proper ethical decisions. Doing ethics in this way also poses several important questions. For example, are these ethical systems adequate for a cohesive society? Christians would respond by saying that those that do not reflect the Creator's purposes are not, because they assume rationality and predictive powers on the part of their proponents and therefore necessarily lack objectivity.

Offering a Critique

Take 'principle' ethics as an example. They are only beneficial if the principles are in fact objectively good. A society may impose a principle that is highly questionable. A given society might dictate that women should be domestic slaves or that children should be compelled into slave labour. Would that society be a moral one simply because it set ethical standards based on principle? Likewise, consequential ethics can be flawed because it is not always possible to determine if an outcome is a good or a bad one. I might feel that abortion is appropriate for a 15-year-old mother-to-be because her education will be adversely affected by having the child, but who is to say that this is actually the case? What if the termination has complications, or she suffers guilt for the rest of her life? Who is to say that this is a better outcome than having a child to love and be devoted to? Moreover, who can determine that the rights of the mother supersede the rights of the unborn child? The mother might argue that it is her right not to be inconvenienced, but does that mean the unborn child does not have a right to life?

And what of the flaws of 'contextual' ethics? We cannot always determine what impact a particular action will have. The Chinese government certainly felt that terminating a second child was good because it controlled the population. However, in practice, girls were terminated rather than boys and now, years later, there is an imbalance in many places between males and females with all the consequences which that entails. Likewise, in the Middle Ages, Europeans in some countries felt the context justified the suppression or forced exile of Jews. Views have clearly changed, but the shifting goal posts bring into question 'contextual' ethics.

'Virtue' ethics are equally flawed, not just because a so-called good person could not possibly be constantly good, but also because it is a subjective assessment to determine that someone is good. There are great people whom we all admire who can make good role models, but only in some aspects of their lives. A rock star might be admired for speaking out against injustice and on behalf of the poor. On the other hand, questions could be asked about his lavish lifestyle and the use of the privilege of his position. Likewise, someone may be considered virtuous, but only because they are not well known. In time they may be seen to be flawed. Someone like the late Jimmy Savile was a much-loved DJ and children's television presenter until the true darkness of his actions was revealed.

It is clear that, without a firm foundation as to the source of truth, each of these ethical models is flawed and therefore can be dangerous. They are not able to offer us a culturally transcendent set of ethical principles free of human subjectivity. The Christian response is to begin by stating that culturally transcendent and objective morals are predicated on the existence of God. If God does indeed exist, and if He is the God described in the Bible, then He is an all-powerful and all-wise being who creates us as human beings and provides us with objective moral standards to live by. Moreover, as our Creator, He knows what is best for us and what will ultimately lead to human flourishing.

Of course, many would object both to the notion that objective moral standards exist in the first place and secondly that a God exists who stands behind these values. The issue of the existence of God is not one for this book, though there are compelling reasons for believing that God does indeed exist.[3] Not only so, and Christians argue that God has spoken into human history and that we have, within the Bible, revealed moral values that are given to the world that are not just useful, but essential, for human flourishing. There are important qualifying statements that also form part of a Christian perspective on ethics. These can be summarised as follows:

- God Himself is a morally perfect being and the values He gives us flow naturally from His person. In other words, they are not detached principles, but values which are intrinsic to His being and reflect His character. What God does is good because God, by His very nature, is good.
- God wants humankind to flourish, and this underlies the values He gives us.

• God is interested in society, its cohesion and wellbeing; this informs these values.
• Every individual is important to God. He loves and desires to protect each person and act for their benefit.

When these statements are seen in the context of the moral values that God demands, they demonstrate that following God's precepts must necessarily be the best for society.

The Growth of Personalised Morality

The most recent direction of travel that can be observed in much of Western society has been the growth of moral relativism. This has meant that there is no consensus about how we should live, no 'one way' which is considered right or the norm, but rather each community deciding for itself what is right and wrong. In this way of thinking, with the exception of some heinous crimes, there is really no such thing as sin. Different forms of behaviour are considered acceptable because they are lifestyle choices; the person who chooses a particular lifestyle decides on their own moral standards. In the words of social scientists Choi and Murphy, 'Each community, accordingly, values certain norms'.[4] In other words, if I behave in a way that you disagree with, you cannot condemn me, because your values come from your interpretive community and my values come from mine. There are no universal standards to which all must adhere.

Moral relativism has the inevitable consequence of reducing ethics to their lowest common denominator. The very lack of any consensus means that there are very few things that we can criticise or even identify as being wrong. As long as you don't hurt anyone or harm nature and you don't judge anyone, you are doing fine from a moral perspective. In such a world, what might in the past have been labelled as sin can no longer be that. It is merely someone's lifestyle choices, it's just 'the way they roll'.

However, in practice it goes farther than that. The 'do not judge others' mantra refers particularly to people's personal lives, their use of leisure time, and especially their personal sexuality. Indeed, human sexuality is a particularly 'sensitive spot' in this new ethical arena. Someone's sexual desires or orientations are personal to the individual and no one has the right to tell another how he or she should behave within the sexual realm. We must accept and celebrate sexual experiences and not judge them. Much the same is true when it comes to what are called 'reproductive rights'. It is entirely up to the individual what they do with their own body, even if this is taken to include an unborn baby.

To raise questions or to set moral parameters on these matters is to be judgmental; such judgmentalism is now seen as the height of intolerance and is itself subject to scrutiny and criticism. As one blogger wryly commented, 'What was condemned is now celebrated, what was celebrated is now condemned, those who refuse to celebrate are condemned.'[5] In such a world traditional moral values, and especially those based on a Judaeo-Christian worldview, are rejected in favour of a new liberal morality.

The New Tyranny

This in turn leads inevitably to a new kind of tyranny, and a double-edged one. On the one hand, for reasons already mentioned, 'political correctness' makes it nearly impossible to critique anyone's lifestyle, behaviour or moral proclivities without being shouted down. Such hectoring has developed its own vocabulary. Words like 'homophobia' and 'transphobia' are now regularly bandied about by those who do not want their lifestyle to be subjected to any rational moral critique.

On the other hand, those same people who call out their moral critics are also inclined to engage in a great deal of their own virtue signalling. They recognise that the direction of travel in public morality has meant that anyone expressing traditional moral values or even advocating free speech in relation to certain subjects is likely to incur wrath from the liberal end of the morality debate. Given this, they often take what they claim is the moral high ground on issues such as sexual expression, feminism, racism, personal liberty and the environment. In a twist of irony, this public discourse has often placed Christians and those who espouse conservative moral values on the defensive in what is a very divisive and unpleasant debate.

For Christians, this is an uncomfortable place to be. It means being treated with intolerance by people who ironically claim they are being tolerant. This agenda of moral relativism will always favour the permissive and condemn those who advocate conservative morality. It is an upside down world in which those who hold to Judaeo-Christian ethics are victimised. As Meic Pearse states, 'the currency of the term tolerance has become badly debased. Where it used to mean the respecting of real, hard difference, it has come to mean instead a dogmatic abdication of claims of truth and a moralistic adherence to moral relativism, departure from either of which is stigmatised as intolerance.'[6]

In this atmosphere free speech is a casualty. There should be space in the public arena to discuss ideas, debating their merits so that some credible answers can be arrived at. However, the vilification of those who dare to question the liberal agenda inevitably shuts down debate.[7] It has led to such phenomena as 'de-platforming' and the creation of so-called 'safe spaces'. The former is an attempt to stifle free speech by ensuring that someone who holds apparently objectionable views is not allowed to express them publicly, either on the street or, for example, on a university campus. The latter is a way of stifling free speech by creating spaces, again often on a university campus or in a working environment, where people are sheltered from views that they might find offensive. Those who act in this way probably feel that they are standing up for some principle. However, they are killing free speech by preventing ideas from being properly debated.

It could also be argued that there is a great deal of the anti-intellectual in these 'progressive' positions. If ideas cannot be discussed and debated properly, feelings often fill the void and become the arbiter of morality. Rather than debating important issues to determine how they should be handled, people increasingly say, 'I feel this is the case', or perhaps, 'this feels right to me'. Emotion replaces reason in our decision-making processes. If, for example, two people are discussing the merits or otherwise of homosexual relationships, the conversation is unlikely to centre on a rational appraisal of the naturalness of same-sex relationships or their advantages for society; rather, it will be based on what the individuals 'feel' about the situation. If they don't feel it is wrong, then it is not. Likewise, if they were discussing the rights and wrongs of sex before marriage, they would not reflect on the positive or negative effects of premarital sex in Western culture, but rather, whether they felt it was OK, and if they felt it was, then it must be so. The problem with this feeling-orientated decision making is that it robs us of any 'fixed point' in discussions. It is a highly volatile and irrational process. Human emotions are fickle at best and can override principles. They are also often self-serving and so bring into our decision making processes an ambiguous and inconsistent method which does not deliver satisfactory answers.

A justification put forward for the morality of the liberal agenda is that it is a more caring way of functioning as a society. If we accept the way in which people choose to live their lives, it is taken as a sign of a loving society. This view is superficial. Just because I choose to accept how people live, that does not constitute a loving act. Indeed, it could well be more loving not to be so accepting of how people live. For example, if someone is abusing their body with dangerous and addictive drugs, telling them the truth about the damage they are doing to themselves is surely a more loving way of treating them.

Not accepting someone's actions can be a way of respecting that person and genuinely wanting what is best for them. It is shallow just to say, 'I will accept whatever you do irrespective of what it is'. It is wiser to say to a person, 'I don't agree with your point of view or your lifestyle, but I love you and value you as a person'. This way of relating to people is much more likely to build genuine and strong relationships and lead to a more coherent society.

Do Objective Ethics Exist?

Do objective ethical values exist, or more to the point, can they exist? The answer to this is 'yes' but this is only because God exists. As long as we keep God out of the picture, we are left in the quagmire of moral relativism. But if we believe in His existence and also recognise that He has given us fixed moral laws to live by, we can find an objective foundation upon which to build our ethics.

The validity of this approach is questioned by our society at large. For Christians, God, as Creator of the universe and everything in it, exercises His supreme authority. Moreover, He has made us morally free beings, able to differentiate in some measure between right and wrong, but also free to choose our own path. The fact that so many people can agree that crimes like murder and rape are wrong is evidence that morals exist. Likewise, the fact that rape and murder do occur is evidence that, although we know what is wrong, we have the freedom to do it anyway. This appeal to a divine law giver makes sense of the world around us.

The presence of a Supreme Being who is sovereign and lays the foundation upon which objective ethical values are built, also means that they are culturally transcendent and unchanging. Something is wrong because God says it is wrong, and it will be wrong at all times and in all places. There is nothing arbitrary about this. It is neither tied to a cultural setting nor a period in history.[8] It is in stark contrast to subjective and changeable ethics and is therefore more secure. The question is, how do we access God's ethical laws? The simple answer is to state that God is a God of self-disclosure. He wants to be known, loved, understood and obeyed.

Primarily this knowledge comes through the historical person of Jesus Christ who revealed God to us through the incarnation. But God's self-disclosure also comes in the pages of the Bible, which is His inspired word. Within Scripture we see ethical commands which are given to help us live constructive lives within a well-functioning community. They teach us self-respect and to respect others and are designed by a loving God to help us and make our lives meaningful. They are brought to a focal point in Exodus 20 where we find the Ten Commandments, which are the foundational building blocks of God's ethical agenda.

Many in our society recoil at any attempt to establish fixed moral laws, arguing that freedom and law are incompatible. However, we know from many areas in life that this is not the case. Rules in sport are necessary for sport to be fun. Likewise, laws on the road make travel safe. In the same way God's laws enhance life rather than hinder it.

Some specifically object to the Ten Commandments on the basis that they are distinctly Christian, or Judaeo-Christian, and therefore irrelevant to anyone who does not espouse that worldview. However, although the Ten Commandments were given to Moses, they had a direct application to the world as a whole. Israel was to be a light to the nations (Isa. 49:6). As God's people lived out these ethical principles, they were to be an example to other nations of a cohesive and successful society.

What is more, the Ten Commandments have been admired by other religious traditions and have been seen by some nations as being of value in guiding their ethical systems. Indeed, it would be hard to find any religious person, or even atheist, who would feel that murder, adultery, theft and dishonesty are good. The Ten Commandments therefore stand as the most obvious ethical model for a world in desperate need of moral guidance.

Notes

[2] M T Nelson, *New Dictionary of Christian Ethics and Pastoral Theology*, p. 253.

[3] Note the 'further reading' guide at the end of this book.

[4] Jung Min Choi and John W Murphy, *The Politics and Philosophy of Political Correctness*, p. 93.

[5] https://www.challies.com/final-call/final-call-january-17/

[6] Meic Pearse, *Why the Rest Hates the West*, p.2.

[7] By 'liberal agenda' I refer to a definite move within Western culture to reject Judaeo-Christian values and oppose the constraints of moral conservatism. I use the term as an expression of philosophy not politics. The so-called liberal agenda is particularly vocal when it comes to issues of human sexuality and reproduction.

[8] A differentiation must be made between the Old Testament laws which God laid down covering 'ethical practice' and those laws that were associated with the particular religious system of Judaism. For example, in saying that God's laws apply at all times, we are referring to ethical laws such as "You shall not commit adultery" (Exod. 20:14); we are not claiming that laws such as the kosher food laws (Deut. 14:8) are applicable to all people at all times.

Chapter 4

Towards a Christian Ethic

Having made the suggestion that the Ten Commandments can form the foundation not only for Christian ethics but also for society as a whole, we now want to look at them in detail and demonstrate their importance. We live in a democracy, not a theocracy, and given the secular nature of our society we need to acknowledge that not all will accept the validity of the Ten Commandments as a credible ethical system, at least initially. However, our laws from the times of King Alfred and later, the Magna Carta, arguably one of the most influential documents in the English-speaking world, have been influenced by Christian belief. Judaeo-Christian values are implicit within our cultural thinking. Christians believe that God created a rational world, and that includes the human beings within it. Consequently, God's moral standards will be consistent with a rational understanding of the natural order that is revealed in creation.[9] If that is the case, then much of Christian thinking, including Christian ethics, can be valued and even endorsed by people who have no religious commitment.

Christians are called to be salt and light (Matt. 5:13-16) and also to seek the welfare of our community (Jer. 29:7). Belief in a Creator who wishes human flourishing should provide Christians with the motivation that is needed to encourage public reflection on the value of the Ten Commandments.

If, as Christians, we believe that the Ten Commandments are credible and that God's value system can work for the benefit of all people, then we should be prepared to argue for them in the public square. In many situations, we may want to avoid discussing the theological background but if we argue our case with rationality, compassion and humility, these values can speak powerfully into our culture. Arguing for them will be both a demonstration that we care for society and an expression of God's purposes. Jesus talked about being as wise as serpents and gentle as doves (Matt. 10:16). These words should inform how we relate to the society around us. We need the courage of our convictions. We should treat everyone, including opponents, with gentleness and respect, and we should have wisdom in knowing when and how to speak into our society.

Introducing the Decalogue

We now turn to the Ten Commandments and consider them in a little more detail. There are two sections to the Ten Commandments, the first being Commandments 1-4 and the second being Commandments 5-10. The first four Commandments are theological in nature and therefore provide a worldview within which all the Commandments are meant to be understood; the remaining six are the ethical components of the Commandments. As Christians we understand that the Commandments all hang together, even though secularists would not relate to the first four. However, given that how we live stems from what we believe, we need to understand and articulate the worldview from which our standards emerge.

The First Commandment

The first four Commandments reveal an inherent respect for God and an orientation of life that is centred around him. The first Commandment demands that we have no other gods in our lives (Exod. 20:3). The second then prohibits the making of any idols (Exod. 20:4). Clearly these fit together and raise the fundamental question as to what we worship in life.

Ancient Israel was surrounded by many pagan nations whose religious life was very different from their own. They were primarily polytheists who worshipped a range of regional deities. Their gods were small in that they occupied a given geographical area rather than being the God of the whole earth whom Israel worshipped (Gen. 18:25; Ps. 139:1-12). Furthermore, these gods were invoked when it came to the many conflicts between warring tribes. If one tribe went to war against another, it was believed that their god would fight against the god of their enemies. Whichever tribe was vanquished, it was a given that their god had been defeated by the rival deity. These gods were not the glorious, holy and all-powerful Jehovah (Jer. 32:27) who loves all people. Rather, they were merely a larger-than-life projection of their worshippers.

Quite apart from the issue of truth, there was a practical and ethical reason why God did not want His people to worship any other gods. It was because there is a link between our behaviour and the thing that we worship. You become like the thing that you worship. As Psalm 135:18 states, 'Those who make them will be like them, and so will all who trust in them'. This point is helpfully summarised by Christian scholar G.K Beale who states, 'People will always reflect something, whether it be God's character or some feature of the world. If people are committed to God, they will become like him; if they are committed to something other than God, they will become like that thing, always spiritually inanimate and empty like the lifeless vain aspect of creation to which they have committed themselves.'[10] This could clearly be seen, for example, in the Canaanites and in their practice of Baal worship. Baal means 'lord', and several of the peoples of the Old Testament world were Baal worshippers. They believed Baal to be a fertility god who was capricious and did not care whom he hurt. He was also sexually promiscuous and objectified people. In the Canaanite 'high places' (places of worship), in order to stimulate their fertility god Baal to have intercourse with his consort Anath, they would emulate him with their own sexual exploits as part of their worship ceremonies. Anath was a goddess of war. According to archaeologist William Albright, she is portrayed as wading up to her neck in the blood of her enemies as she trampled on their skulls and decorated herself with human heads.[11] The Canaanites were a people whose atrocities, even against their own children, were outrageous in the extreme, but were an inherent part of their theology. Their belief system gave them permission to live as they did. What they believed about their god replicated itself in their own lives. A modern version of this might be seen in extremist Muslims belonging to groups like ISIS, who behave in a way that reflects what they believe theologically.

It is for this reason the Ten Commandments begin with the command to have no other gods. If God were to allow polytheism, there would be little possibility of ensuring that His people were holy and had regard for biblical ethics.

The Second Commandment

The second Commandment prohibits the making of any idol. This is a subtly different issue, but one that reminds us of the need to be cautious about what we value in life. An idol is essentially something that we make more important in our lives than God. What we elevate in life could be something tangible such as a car, a career, leisure time or property. Equally it could be something abstract like self-image, fame or celebrity.

The danger is that idols can distort. They have the capacity to alter our value system and make us see the world from a wrong perspective. It is not hard to grasp how this can impact on ethics. When we worship and make idols of material possessions, we devalue other important things, such as other people. It can skew our priorities so that we make bad decisions.

Likewise, we can make an idol of celebrity and allow that to colour our thinking. In popular culture, people might criticise politicians for the money they earn, or hold them to an unreasonably high standard and criticise them when they fail. However, when a celebrity makes an enormous amount of money and lives a highly promiscuous life, the same standards might not be applied. Idols disfigure, and only when we shun idols can we have a clear perspective on life.

The Third and Fourth Commandments

When it comes to the third and fourth Commandments, they are profound because of what they imply. The third Commandment demands that we do not misuse God's name (Exod. 20:7). Of course, this speaks to the cheapening of sincerely held religious faith by using God's name as a swear word. But there is much more to it. At the heart of this command there is the whole issue of integrity. In the ancient world people made promises by invoking the name of their god. This was in effect a guarantee of honesty, rather like when people today might use a casual expression like 'I swear to God'. The real problem, however, was that dishonesty was as rife as it is today. People would make promises that they had no intention of keeping. In order to add weight to their promises, they would invoke the name of their god in the hope they would be believed. In effect, this cheapened both the promise and the name of that god.

In the context of this command, God was forbidding His name to be used in this way. If someone were to make a promise, that promise needed to be kept. Their word should be trusted simply because the person had integrity. The same command is repeated in Leviticus 19:12 and Jeremiah 5:2, demonstrating that from God's perspective this was important. Likewise, Jesus told us not to make oaths, but for our 'yes' to be yes and 'no' to be no (Matt. 5:33-37). He was not calling for oaths to be abandoned altogether but rather, He demanded that honesty and integrity be hallmarks of His followers.[12]

We can see how these relate to ethics. Conversation and debate about ethics is not possible unless there is a commitment to telling the truth. Without integrity individual lives and society cannot function properly. The opposite of integrity is corruption and the opposite of honesty is dishonesty. There must be honesty and integrity when it comes to the promises we make in life. It should be implicit in contracts and it should apply to our obligation to the State to pay our taxes.

The fourth Commandment is to keep the Sabbath holy (Exod. 20:8). This is the only Commandment that Jesus did not explicitly repeat in the gospels. However, there is an important principle at stake. When we look at the creation story, we note that God laboured for six days, and on the seventh He rested. This was clearly a template for humanity. This Commandment made the Sabbath a day of rest from work. It was an expression of God's care for humanity that He ensured there would be a time for rest and recuperation.

This was almost certainly unique in the ancient world. Life for all but the very wealthy was drudgery. Whether you were a farmer or a trader, a slave or a hired hand, life consisted of long, hard, often very physically taxing days. For ordinary people it was constant backbreaking grind with no let-up. Then God spoke into the culture of Israel and gave this command for a day of rest. This was the first true 'holyday'.

Life today can also be demanding. Many people are compelled to work under constant pressure, driving up productivity, maximising profits, but often at the expense of their health and family life. The consumerism of our culture entices us to buy products that we don't need and in turn we work damaging hours to pay for them. This commandment gives a sense of perspective, valuing the person more than the product and recognising that human life consists of more than just commercial pursuits.

Dealing with Specific Values

We now come to the commands that specifically relate to ethical issues. It is not surprising that the first of these (the fifth Commandment) relates to family values. After all, the family is the basic unit of society and, if this breaks down, society as a whole begins to crumble. Often when issues such as anti-social behaviour are being publicly debated, people will blame government austerity, the lack of police numbers and the closure of youth centres. These have a bearing. However, more important may be poor parenting, absent fathers and the fragmentation of family life. There have been numerous reports on the effect of family breakdown, though these are not reflected in government policy, due to the fear of stigmatising the affected families.[13]

The Commandment specifies that we are to honour our father and mother (Exod. 20:12). We should not forget that Jesus Himself was obedient to this and modelled it. The first thirty years of His life were lived in His home village and, if we assume that Joseph died prematurely (after all he is not mentioned in John 2:1-11), then Jesus, as the eldest son, had the responsibility to act as head of family, something which He clearly carried out. We even see Him on the cross ensuring that His mother would be cared for (John 19:26-27).

This Commandment illuminates a surprising angle. Rather than urging parents to control their children, the command is to children to have due respect for their parents. There are two reasons for this. Firstly, it is easier to give orders than to take them, so the Commandment deals with the more difficult issue. Secondly, the family unit only works when submission is willingly given. Parents of course have a huge role to play, but the focus here is on the issue of children honouring their parents. This poses the question, what does it mean to honour parents?

In the first place it involves gratitude. The simple fact that parents generally make great sacrifices for children and put in such hard work to care for and raise them, is deserving of honour. However, gratitude is often not shown. This can be true of contemporary Western culture where some old people are considered an inconvenience and put away in 'eventide' homes. Other cultures, where more old people are looked after in families, have something to teach us here. We need genuinely to express gratitude to our parents for their unconditional love if we are to begin obeying this Commandment.

Secondly, there is the matter of obedience. Every child needs to respect the values their parents teach them, as the home is their first school. Parents, children and indeed governments need to recognise this. There will inevitably come a time when a child is old enough to be independent and to act autonomously. Contemporary culture has put pressure on families to encourage children at younger ages to express that freedom. Young people are encouraged to make some decisions about life at a point when they do not have the maturity to do so. This has not been helped by parents who abrogate their responsibility to exercise control over their children, which has led to unruly behaviour by some young people. Part of the role of the church as a force for good in society should be to support families and encourage young people to be obedient to parents.

Parents need to earn respect (Col. 3:20-21) and they do this through loving and patient parenting based on relationship. Parents must also help their children develop towards independence. Nevertheless, obedience is a requirement, especially in our contemporary culture where discipline in the home is often neglected.

What should happen when children grow up and establish their own families? Should I as a 53-year-old father of three with a career and mortgage still obey my parents? Clearly the answer is no. However, I should still be willing to listen and give regard to their wisdom. Support is also part of honouring parents and this too is often reflected better in non-Western parts of the world. Western society has tended to allow the State to take over some of the responsibilities that a family should have. While we should be grateful for those social services and make use of them, they should not detract from our own responsibilities. Ageing parents should be helped and supported through this difficult part of their lives, not ignored, disrespected and certainly not euthanised.

We should notice how this Commandment ends. The result of obedience, 'that you may live long in the land' (v. 12), is a highly instructive one. Israel as a young nation had many enemies. The only way they could survive would be by building a strong and cohesive society. Family was essential to this. If, in the UK, we allow family life to disintegrate further, one wonders what future challenges our culture would be able to cope with.

The Value of Life

The sixth Commandment, 'You shall not murder' (Exod. 20:13), speaks for itself. Most people believe in the value of human life and would recognise that killing is bad. In the majority of countries, if one human being unlawfully kills another, they are punished. However, we live in a world that is complex.

We need to remind ourselves that we are made in the image of God (Gen. 1:28) and therefore each one of us, at whatever stage of life, is of intrinsic value. No other aspect of creation is described this way; we, as human beings, are special and unique. Even if someone is not religious, they see that humans are of a different category of life from animals. This is why, as we have mentioned earlier, when we see a lion killing a gazelle on the plains of the Serengeti, we do not describe it as murder, but when a person kills another, we do. Human life is a precious commodity and we do not have the moral authority to decide who lives or dies.

We should note that the Commandment states 'Do not murder'. Clearly, we need a working definition of what 'murder' is, because it is not exactly the same as taking a life. Moreover, it may be defined slightly differently depending on the country or culture. For example, a soldier could be sent to war (perhaps a just war) and in combat could take life. This would not be murder. Likewise, there could be a situation where a person is responsible for a genuine accident, for example a car crash in which someone dies, but this would not be murder, not least because it was not intentional. Someone who represents the State, like a policeman or a member of the security services, could also be in a situation where, in carrying out their job, perhaps apprehending a violent criminal, they have to take a life. This would not be murder if they were acting in a legitimate way on behalf of the State in a role that keeps people safe.[14] Doctors too may need to take difficult decisions in situations where, for instance, people are being kept alive artificially even though it is clear that they are essentially brain dead.

We could say that murder is the deliberate taking of a human life without justification. From a Christian perspective, all life belongs to God and human life is special and valued. Given the caveats mentioned, it should be clear that neither an individual nor the State has the right to take life without good cause.

The Foundation of Marriage

The seventh Commandment brings us back to the arena of family and focuses specifically on the importance of the marriage relationship. It states, 'You shall not commit adultery' (Exod. 20:14). Marriage is an ancient practice and is respected all over the world. The sanctity of marriage is so important in Scripture that this command is repeated many times in both the Old and New Testaments. If family life begins to collapse, so too does society, since the family is the basic unit of society. And the married relationship is the foundation of family life.

There are those who debate the utility of marriage, but the evidence shows that the institution of marriage is good for society. This Commandment therefore offers protection to marriage by speaking against the most obvious threat to a marriage, which is when one partner begins an illicit sexual relationship with someone outside the marriage. In popular culture the expression, 'it's just sex' is used in order to minimise the seriousness of the act. However, it is more than that because human beings are complex, and we know that we have a sensitive emotional life that can easily be damaged. Adultery is a betrayal: it robs the relationship of trust, it causes great pain and it is a denial of the marriage vow. The Bible views marriage as sacred and anything that would undermine it is serious.

Personal Property

The eighth Commandment states 'You shall not steal' (Exod. 20:15). Again, this is one that people recognise as being important, because in almost all cultures theft[15] is wrong and does damage to society. Without a prohibition against theft, society could not function.

The temptation as well as the opportunity to steal may be greater than ever. The open style of modern shops makes shoplifting easier. The use of modern technology has also assisted thieves and broadened the range of goods and even ideas that can be stolen. Evading legitimate taxes, which is stealing from the State, has become common (this should not be confused with tax avoidance, which is lawful, but for many, in its extreme forms, wrong.) But there are other matters akin to theft which we do not often think about.

There is the 'theft' of time. When someone accepts a job they enter into a contract of employment and that needs to be honoured. The expectation is that the person will work for a certain number of hours per day. In reality, it is common for employees to shave time off the day. It may be done by taking longer lunch and tea breaks, coming in late and leaving early.

There can also be 'theft' of character. Sometimes the most valuable thing a person has is their character and reputation. It is possible through gossip or slander to ruin it and, when this is done deliberately, it is a form of theft in a moral sense (rather than a strict legal sense). Even if it is just done through carelessness, it can still be serious and have the same impact.

The Truth and the Whole Truth

The ninth Commandment relates to the things that people might say. It states, 'You shall not bear false witness' (Exod. 20:16). Like many of the commands, it is repeated in the same form in Deuteronomy 5:20. The expression 'false witness' is an interesting one because it is a legal term. It would be used of someone giving testimony in a court of law.[16] If witnesses in court give false evidence, the court could reach a wrong verdict, and the process of law would be perverted.

More than that, as the Commandments relate to everyday life, it is clear that, as far as God is concerned, there is no such thing as casual speech. Everything we say is of importance and we are accountable for what we say. We would generally be much more careful giving testimony in court than we would speaking in everyday life, but that does not remove our obligation to be honest in all our dealings. Proverbs 6:19 states that God hates, 'a false witness who pours out lies'.

In the New Testament, we see Jesus describing sins that emerge from a heart of evil, among them false witness (Matt. 15:19). We see this sin in action against Jesus (Matt. 26:59-60) and Stephen (Acts 6:13). If what we say about others is not true, this stems from a corrupted heart. The point of this Commandment is that it requires truthfulness from all, and in every context and situation. It demands that, whatever we say, it must be the truth and we should not make any attempt to mislead.

Implicit in this Commandment is something that is articulated later in Leviticus 5:1: 'If anyone sins because they do not speak up when they hear a public charge to testify regarding something they have seen or learned about, they will be held responsible'. This is challenging. If someone hears something being said that is false and does nothing to expose the untruth, that person is culpable even if they have not lied themselves. If we do not do so in circumstances when our silence will be taken for agreement it is, in effect, similar to lying (although not quite the same). The moral imperative is not only to refrain from saying wrong things, but positively to promote truth.

There are many ways in which lies emerge. Some lies come out of bitterness and usually manifest themselves in slander or gossip. It is easy to take revenge on someone by what we say about them. When describing people, we can embellish our negative descriptions of them. We may be saying some things about them that are true, but adding our own 'spin' using language in clever and subtle ways, which have the effect of conveying an impression that is not true.

There are also lies that stem from fear. Even children do this instinctively if confronted by someone questioning them about whether they have done something they should not have. However, adults also do the same thing and in a more sophisticated but nevertheless deliberate way. It is an easy temptation to distort the truth if doing so protects us from criticism or accusation, where the impression given is still false and a breach of this Commandment.

Lies can also emerge for personal gain. Many people will automatically be sceptical when confronted by a salesman of a product, because they assume that the truth will be massaged in some way in order to get a sale. In many walks of life, it is possible to gain advantage by being economical with the truth. This makes the ninth Commandment one of the most often broken.

Wanting What Doesn't Belong to You

The tenth and final Commandment states, 'You shall not covet' (Exod. 20:17). It is interesting because it does not involve a physical action but rather, an attitude. Thoughts can lead to actions, but this command requires us not to wish for or desire something that does not legitimately belong to us. Characters in the Old Testament such as Achan (Josh. 7:20-21) demonstrate examples of this problem.

The issue is not the object that we covet but the coveting itself. This can manifest itself in all kinds of ways. We can covet material possessions, which can be a driver in our lives. Hence Paul declared in 1 Timothy 6:10 that 'the love of money is a root of all kinds of evil'. However, we can also covet less tangible things like social status. Indeed, the desire for prominence is a fundamental part of human nature. The Pharisees came under Jesus' scrutiny because of this (Matt. 23:5-7), as did His disciples, James and John, who were angling for better positions (Mark 10:35-45). Coveting can lead to envy and jealousy, which inevitably destroy community life. It is also possible to covet a person, hence the command, 'Do not covet your neighbour's wife' (Exod. 20:17). It is not difficult to see how destructive this could be.

The best way to deal with coveting is to be content with what we have and to be willing to work hard and with integrity to gain what we need.

These then are the Ten Commandments or Decalogue. They form the basis of the Judaeo-Christian worldview. They were given to Israel, but this was only part of the story. Israel was meant to be a light to the nations (Isa. 42:6). The Ten Commandments enabled them to live this out. The world would then be able to adopt these values and live them out as well. Part of our responsibility as Christians should be to commend them to society. With the failure of all other ethical models, the benefits of the Christian way should be promoted.

Notes

[9] John Scriven, *Belief and the Nation*, p. 121.

[10] G K Beale, We Become What We Worship: A Biblical Theology of Idolatry, p. 284.

[11] W F Albright, *Archaeology and the Religion of Israel*, p. 77.

[12] Matthew 26:63 tells us that Jesus did not refuse to give an answer under oath.

[13] https://www.centreforsocialjustice.org.uk/library/fractured-families-stability-matters

[14] This is a particularly complex example because there could be situations in which a given State might sanction a killing which might be seen as a contravention of 'international law'. In other words, the State's involvement does not necessarily guarantee that this would be a legitimate use of lethal force.

[15] It should be noted that the legal definition of theft can vary from country to country. In the UK the strict definition is narrower than the examples given here, though there are other criminal offences relating to dishonest gain. We are talking here about theft in a broader sense.

[16] P C Craigie, *The Book of Deuteronomy*, p. 162.

Chapter 5

Abortion – the Slaughter of the Innocent

Having reflected on the place of Christian ethics in our society at large, we now turn to some specific issues where Christians offer a different perspective to that which is now generally accepted. We will deal with three contentious issues which all relate to our human sexuality. They are: abortion, traditional marriage and transgenderism.

We begin with the challenging issue of abortion, made all the more important by the sheer number of unborn children whose lives are cut short through deliberate action.

Defining the Term

Put simply, abortion is the ending of the life of an embryo or a foetus after implantation in the mother's womb. In Great Britain, abortions could only be carried out in hospitals and clinics. Now, medical abortions can take place at home using the current pandemic as justification. This change could become permanent. Guidelines state that the pregnant woman is to be assessed prior to an abortion so she may talk it through with clinicians and a trained counsellor.[17] The two methods of abortions used are 'medical' and 'surgical'.

Medical abortion

This procedure is normally carried out up to 10 weeks into the pregnancy and tends to carry a lower risk for the woman. A medical abortion involves taking medication to end the pregnancy; this method does not require surgery or anaesthetic. The mother first takes mifepristone, which blocks the hormone that facilitates pregnancy. Around 24 or 48 hours later the mother takes misoprostol. This will break down the lining of the womb, causing bleeding and the end of the pregnancy. If the medical abortion takes place after nine weeks, there may be a need for several doses of misoprostol. Sometimes the foetus and placenta do not pass, so a surgical intervention is required.

Surgical abortion

Surgical abortions are normally done between 10 and 13 weeks into the pregnancy and later abortions after 18 weeks. Later abortions involve a combination of medical and surgical interventions with the use of suction and forceps. A surgical abortion involves a procedure under local anaesthetic and sometimes general anaesthetic. Two methods are used:

• Vacuum or suction aspiration, which can be used up to 15 weeks into the pregnancy. Here a tube is inserted into the womb and the pregnancy is brought to an end with the foetus being removed using suction. The procedure takes just a few minutes.

• Dilation and evacuation (D&E), which is used from around 15 weeks into the pregnancy. This procedure uses forceps to bring an end to the pregnancy and remove the foetus.

Later abortions after 22 weeks are rare and are generally carried out due to severe foetal abnormality. They are a two-stage process where potassium is injected into the foetal heart to extinguish life and then either labour is induced or a surgical termination with general anaesthetic is performed.

Abortion is legal up to 24 weeks and up to birth if there is a substantial risk that if the child were born it would suffer from such physical or mental abnormalities as to be seriously handicapped.

A Sizeable Challenge

Since the Abortion Act (1967) came into force, there have been over 9 million abortions in the UK.[18] Figures for 2017 show that less than 1% were because the mother's life was at risk, while 2% were carried out on the grounds of foetal disability.[19] The vast majority were for reasons associated with mental health, which are assumed to be mainly social reasons.

The rise in the rate of abortions shows no signs of abating. An article in The Independent newspaper in June of 2019 suggested that in England

and Wales the abortion rate had reached an all-time high of 200,000 per year.[20] The report also revealed that the recent rise was caused by older women seeking abortions. Abortion is not something that a person might do only once, at a point of real crisis, and never again. The reality is that in 2016 some 38% of women in England and Wales who had abortions had previously undergone one or more abortions.[21] Of these, 1047 women had obtained four previous abortions while 58 of them had obtained eight or more abortions. Clearly the law has opened a wide door which many take advantage of.

One of the political issues that relates to the Abortion Act is the number of weeks into the pregnancy at which abortion is permitted. In the UK it is allowed for social reasons up to 24 weeks into the pregnancy, which is among the most liberal pieces of abortion legislation in Europe. (Several European countries set the limit at 12 weeks.) Given that babies born under 24 weeks can survive and are cared for in neo-natal units in hospitals, it is inconsistent that at the same time in the same hospitals healthy babies of similar age are being aborted. Foetuses can feel pain well below the 24-week limit. Indeed, major studies indicate that unborn children can feel pain at between 16 and 18 weeks and possibly even from eight weeks' gestation.[22]

The Health of the Mother

There are the potentially damaging effects that abortion can cause for the mother. Despite protests to the contrary, there is substantial evidence that the risks can be serious. The first is the possibility of mental illness. Studies show that women having induced abortions are twice as likely to suffer mental health problems, three times as likely to have depression and six times as likely to commit suicide, as mothers who do not have an abortion.[23] Moreover, numerous studies have also found that women who have had an abortion are more likely to have subsequent premature births and that this risk increases with repeated abortions.[24] Whilst there is evidence of adverse effects on mental health from abortion, there is also evidence of existing mental illness in some women seeking abortion, as well as, for some, the risk of perinatal mental illness for those who continue with a pregnancy.

There is also evidence that the procedure itself can have complications.

These are spelled out on the NHS website.[25] It states that 1 in 10 women having an abortion contracts an infection in the womb, and that in 1 in 20 cases some contents from the pregnancy remain in the womb. The website also states that in some cases the pregnancy continues, requiring further treatment. Excessive bleeding which may require blood transfusions can occur in 1 in 1000 cases, and damage to the cervix can happen in 1 in 100 cases. Damage can also be done to the womb in 1 in every 250 cases where a surgical abortion is carried out and 1 in every 1000 cases with medical abortions. It can be argued that a woman is doing this to her own body and not to someone else. Nevertheless, women seeking abortions need to know that the invasiveness of abortion is risky and that they may suffer regret afterwards.

Whatever our views about the morality of individual abortions, the number of abortions that now take place should cause us as a society to ask if this is a social good. It is concerning that very few voices are ever raised which question abortion, particularly among pastors and clergy. Bishop Michael Nazir-Ali said in March 2020 (quoted in The British Church Newspaper): 'The government statistics reveal that we are looking a demographic disaster in the face' and went on to say, 'Our primary concern has to be about the large scale destruction of humans ... who have no voice for themselves.'

When concerns are raised there is often a furious reaction. This was typified by a recent incident in which Labour MP Stella Creasy protested at a billboard showing a 9-week-old living foetus, posted by campaign group CBR UK.[26] The group's purpose is to challenge public opinion on the issue of abortion by educating the public as to the humanity of the unborn child. They do so by getting people to look at the facts and come up with their own informed opinion. The mere fact of the billboard caused Creasy to respond angrily on Twitter calling the billboard 'crap' and inferring that it constituted the harassment of women. It seems a strange description given that the group's motivation is to protect human life.

A Clash of Opinions and Rights

Abortion presents a clash of opinions and rights, and one that pits two sides against each other. Those who favour the legalisation of abortion would not describe themselves as pro-abortion but rather 'pro-choice'. For them the issue is not the abortion itself, but rather the right of a woman to choose what to do with her own body and its reproductive organs. They place a high value on personal freedom and argue that it should be the woman's right to choose what to do with both her life and that of her unborn child, and to take control of her 'reproductive destiny'. For them, restrictions on abortion curtail a woman's rights and denies her the liberty to choose what happens to her own body.

Other issues raised are those of the safety of the mother and the health of the baby. There are of course situations (such as ectopic pregnancies) where the mother's life can be put at risk because of the pregnancy, and pro-choice advocates argue that the woman should have the right to bring the pregnancy to an end because of the threat to her life and health. There is also the health of the child. If it is discovered that the child will be born with some serious mental or physical defect, then the impact on the woman's life, and indeed on her whole family, will be significant. Again, it is argued that she must have the right to make a choice as to whether she continues with the pregnancy and has the child or not. Once again, her rights and the ability to make choices that affect her future are paramount in the argument.

Added to these central arguments are ancillary but highly emotionally-charged ones. What should happen in a case where a woman is raped and becomes pregnant, or in a case where she becomes pregnant because of incest? Once again, her choice, it is argued, should be paramount. The mental and emotional turmoil of such events are horrendous. Activists cite the anguish that is added to every day that the pregnancy continues. They claim that it ought to be her choice as to what to do with her own body, and to deny her this would be a cruel infringement of her freedom.

Some pro-choice advocates take an even more radical line, arguing that abortion is more than just a human right, it is a positive moral good. Psychologist and writer Valerie Tarico takes this position, boldly stating that she is not just pro-choice but pro-abortion.[27] She goes on to explain that she is in favour of abortion, just as she is in favour of knee replacements or cataract operations, because it is part of a set of tools that helps women and men to enhance their lives by forming the families of their choosing. She notes that it involves choosing some of your children to live while choosing others to die, but this is justified on that basis that she loves the children that she has chosen and all their lives are better for it.

On the Horns of a Dilemma

When pro-choice arguments are heard, some can sound compelling. The freedom of the individual, along with the traumatic circumstances of some conceptions, elicit sympathy and understanding for the pro-abortion case. In practice, pro-choice and pro-life advocates often 'shout past' each other, because both are concerned with the issue of rights and both believe they have a valid argument. The validity or otherwise of their arguments needs to be debated. It is a debate that requires both careful handling and the ability to stand back from the emotion and ask searching questions about the reality behind the theory.

To start with, we can ask some important subsidiary questions. The first of these is: should men have any rights when it comes to the issue of abortion? This is a question that can evoke anger. Some women have argued that abortion is about their body as they are the carrier of the foetus, so it should be their decision alone as to whether the baby should be kept or not.

It is true that it is the woman who goes through all the experiences related to pregnancy. Equally it is true that, when a child is not wanted, the man can and, often does, walk away leaving the woman responsible for the consequences. The difficulty and loneliness of this situation cannot be overestimated, and a man should be held accountable for any child conceived. No man has the right to father a child and abandon the woman with whom he had the child. That notwithstanding, it is wrong to claim that decisions about the child should only be that of the woman. True, she is primarily responsible since she carries the child through the pregnancy. However, no child could be conceived without a man; that fact alone should confer on him some right of decision-making, but only if he chooses to be involved in the child's life.

Another question is the issue of children conceived by rape or incest. While some abortions are carried out on these grounds, the vast majority are carried out for social convenience. In debate, pro-choice advocates turn quickly to these emotive issues and use them as a pretext to allow for the widespread use of abortion.

Rape is an abhorrent crime, as is incest. However, in relation to the abortion issue these crimes represent only a tiny percentage of abortions. They do not justify the very many babies that are terminated for reasons of social convenience. It is a false argument to justify these abortions on the tragic reality of rape and incest. Even in a case such as rape there are not just two, but three, people involved. There is the rapist whose deeds are evil and despicable. There is the woman who is innocent and has been treated terribly. But there is also the child who is equally innocent and is as much a victim of circumstances as his or her mother. We cannot ignore the rights of the child, including its right to life.

When Does Human Life Begin?

We now come to the most important question that needs to be asked: when does human life begin? The morality of abortion is fundamentally bound up with this question. We would not think of taking the life of a baby or a toddler, because we recognise that they are human. In what sense then is a foetus any different? In Scotland the irony of the situation is even more apparent. Recently the Scottish Parliament banned the smacking of children, while abortion is permitted. That means you can terminate the life of a child within the womb, but you cannot smack a child once it is born.

For some, an embryo in its mother's womb has the potential to 'become' a human life, but it cannot be considered to be human until some point in the pregnancy. Opinions on exactly when that point is vary from one person to another and often shift depending on cultural pressure. The problems with this view are threefold. First, the embryo is clearly a living thing that is developing fast and is not just some inanimate object. Secondly, the embryo is already genetically human, containing human DNA, and is therefore incapable of developing into anything other than a human being. Thirdly, while it may not look recognisably human early on, it will do so increasingly and in a matter of weeks, and the transition into a fully-fledged human is inevitable. The only thing that will stop this from happening, other than something going wrong with the pregnancy, is the termination of its life.

Others respond to this issue by stating that humanity is defined by particular human functions that need to be in place. They would say that until the embryo or the foetus manifests these functions, it should not be treated as fully human. These functions may vary depending on who is arguing the case. Moreover, they might include the ability to communicate and the ability to form relationships. This argument is fraught with difficulties because the same could be said of other children. It could be argued that a new born baby does not fulfil the criteria and so infanticide is morally acceptable. Likewise, a severely disabled person, someone in a coma, or a comatose elderly person might fail the test, so on this argument, ending their lives ought not to cause any moral concern.

A similar argument is used by people who see 'humanness' developing in a gradual way. As an embryo becomes a foetus and then as the foetus grows and develops, so its humanness develops over a period of time. This time period need not just be confined to the womb. Indeed, ethicist Peter Singer suggests that a baby of several weeks can still be terminated if it does not sufficiently demonstrate normal human attributes. This argument also fails because it is so arbitrary. Some argue that the embryo becomes biologically significant at 14 days. Others suggest that the limit ought to be set at 24 weeks and others still at 28 weeks and, as mentioned, Peter Singer applies the limit to a point well after the birth of the baby. With such an arbitrary evaluation, who can know what is right? This gradualist approach is both biologically and philosophically problematic. After all, what is the difference between a 24-week-old child and a child that is 23 weeks and 6 days old.

If none of these answers is satisfying, what should the answer be? The best and most compelling approach is to say that the human life begins at conception and should be regarded as a human person from that point. There are several reasons for this. First, the new organism that fertilisation has produced is distinct from any other cell in the mother and the father and not equivalent to any of the mother's eggs or the father's sperm. Consequently, it is not just a collection of tissue, but rather a distinct entity and being.[28]

Secondly, it is clear that the organism is human. It is not, nor will it be, any other form of life or being. It is the product of a human mother and a human father and contains exclusively the genetic makeup of human beings. That brings us to the third and related point. The new zygote, which will soon transform into an embryo, is a whole human being. It is, of course, microscopic because it is at such an early stage of development. However, the lack of maturity, which is part of the natural process, cannot mask the fact that an entire human being exists there. Unlike the sperm or the egg which each contains only half the genetic material needed to produce a human being, the zygote contains it all. If it is given the support it needs, it already contains all the internal apparatus and genetic material to bring itself to full maturity.

It must also be stated that the zygote and then the embryo will develop by itself if allowed to. Of course, it will be reliant on the mother who carries this life, and at such an early stage of development it will have no possibility of survival outside the womb. Nevertheless, with the support and nurture of the mother, the embryo will develop; everything necessary is already in place to create a human baby. Once this process is underway, unless something goes medically wrong, or there is intervention from the outside, that zygote will become an embryo and then form, inevitably, into a fully-fledged human being. Given the potentiality, it is most logical to conclude that human life has begun. That being the case, any attempt to end the progress of life by deliberate and unnatural means must be recognised as such, with all the ethical implications that this brings.

It could be argued that a case can be made for the notion of life beginning slightly later, at the point of implantation because this is the point when the pregnancy becomes viable. Those who argue this case do so on the basis of what they perceive to be a wasteful situation, when many zygotes are lost between fertilisation and implantation. While this position is understandable, the life in the form of an adult, teenager, child, infant, foetus, embryo, blastocyst and zygote are all stages of development of a human organism. Moreover, we would not apply the 'natural wastage' argument to people in general, so it would be inconsistent to apply it in this situation. If this concession were to be made it would be a relatively small one since implantation occurs within days of fertilisation.

What science supports, the Bible teaches. There are a number of key passages that focus on this issue. Psalm 139:13-14 speaks of God being actively involved in the process of creating a human being. Then in

Psalm 51:5 David speaks about being sinful or fallen at the time of his conception. In the words of Carl Laney, 'this indicates that the moral law of God was already present and operative in his pre-natal state. Since Scripture attributes moral guilt to David as an unborn child, it follows that he was human before birth'.[29]

What about Personhood?

Even when presented with the scientific evidence, pro-choice advocates have an answer, and that is to make a distinction between being 'human' and being a 'person'. They attempt to negate the ethical implications of abortion by stating that while a child in the womb may be a human being, it is not necessarily a person. If an unborn child is a non-person, it is ethically permissible to terminate its life.

From a theological angle this is certainly wrong. Ultimately, we are made in the image of God and created as unique individuals. Our personhood and ultimate value are derived from the image of Himself that God has given us. God forms us individually and has a purpose for what we are to be. Indeed, God loved us and had a plan for us before our birth and even before the creation of the world (Jer. 1:5; 2 Tim. 1:9), so in that sense we were persons even before our conception. Not that we actually existed before conception, but that the God who knows everything already had a plan for us and then created us at our conception so that we could live out the plan He had for our lives. It is therefore wrong to deny personhood to the unborn. Having said this, we should also reflect on the issue of personhood from a philosophical perspective.

What is a Person?

The denial of the personhood of an unborn child is nothing new. Peter Singer and liberal Catholic theologian Hans Kung are two examples of thinkers who take the position that humanness and personhood are separate.[30] Generally, those who take this view state that personhood is some kind of acquired characteristic that a human being develops over time. For example, the human being must be in some way self-aware, or have some other characteristic, in order to have personhood. This might call into question the personhood of a severely disabled or even comatose adult. The beginning point of personhood is necessarily arbitrary and self-referential, rather than being based on some clearly defined criteria. Given what is at stake, we should require a much more compelling reason for denying personhood to the unborn.

Against the theory of personhood as a justification for abortion is that personhood is not a quality, such as intelligence, which can vary from one person to another and, even less so is it a changeable characteristic such as the colour of our hair. Rather, personhood should be seen as an essential quality of a human being. In other words, it is not possible to be human without being a person. One automatically means the other. There are compelling reasons for saying this. First, if we refuse to grant personhood to someone until they reach some imaginary bar of intellectual ability or some other quality, then using that rationale, it could be argued that there might be circumstances in which it would be morally acceptable to kill a healthy six-week-old baby because it had limited or as yet undeveloped intellectual abilities.

In addition, within nature there is a distinction, but at the same time a connection, between the actual and the potential. Whatever quality the personhood deniers set as a barrier, this distinction and connection applies. The difference is one of degree, the connection is one of essential nature. Take the quality of intellectual development as an example. That same six-week-old baby has gone through more intellectual development than a foetus, but less than a twenty-year-old. The difference is in degree, but the commonality is the quality of 'human' intelligence. If allowed to live and therefore develop, the human being will develop human intelligence and not any other kind of intelligence, with all that this means. This is because, innately, it is potentially there. Even if illness or disability might prevent or impair development, the potentiality that exists is human potentiality. These are degrees within a continuum, but at every point the nature is human. Moreover, each human with this potentiality will be a unique individual; no two humans are exactly alike. The link between what is potential and what exists allows no justification for separating the humanity of an embryo, foetus or unborn child from its personhood. We do not become a human person by degrees – full humanity is an inherent part of the life that comes about through fertilisation, complete with all the genetic information needed to develop as a human being.

It's My Body – I can do what I Like

Even when the argument for the humanity and personhood of the baby is accepted, many pro-choice advocates still argue that a woman ought to have the right to do what she likes with her own body. This argument can sound compelling, but it is still based on a false premise. Even if it were granted that a woman could do what she wanted with her own body (and that is still debatable), the foetus inside her is not her own body. Indeed, the placenta and umbilical cord which separate the foetus from the mother are evidence of this separation.[31] The baby has its own circulatory and nervous system and, while it is dependent on the mother for protection and nourishment, it is nevertheless a completely different being. From an ethical point of view therefore, if the mother has an abortion it is not her body she is specifically harming, it is the life of the child she carries. That child's humanity and personhood makes such an act a serious ethical violation.

In the complex world in which we live, people's perceived 'rights' are often in conflict and difficult decisions have to be made. The fact that unborn children are real persons means that their rights also have to be respected. Their vulnerability also means that others have to speak for them, as they are unable to speak for themselves. In this situation, the mother's 'rights' have to be considered in the context of the child's right to life and to be loved and cared for. Particularly given that most abortions are performed for social reasons, because the child is unwanted or inconvenient, the child's rights must surely be recognised.

Rape and Incest

Returning to the sensitive issues of the possible justification of abortion in the case of rape or incest, these are (as mentioned above) used as part of the argument for allowing abortion, even though only a very small percentage of abortions are requested based on rape or incest. Nevertheless, we cannot ignore either the seriousness of these issues or the excruciating trauma women suffer as a result of these two evils.

While these acts are undoubtedly evil and deserving of punishment for the perpetrator, the child conceived is not the guilty party. It is therefore unjust that they should forfeit their right to life for the wrongs of others. Moreover, if abortion is morally wrong (and the case presented so far would suggest that it is), it seems strange that we could justify using a morally wrong act as a response to an evil act. Two wrongs do not balance out to make something right.

We have already noted that abortion is not without its complications for the women involved. There is no way of knowing that the termination will not add to the psychological trauma that they will already be experiencing. We need to recognise that in cases as difficult and complex as this there are no quick fixes.

Pro-choice advocates argue that forcing a woman, who has already suffered the profound trauma of rape or incest, to carry the child full term would be adding even more suffering to a situation which is already unbearable. This is of course true, but it does not solve the complexity of the situation. While allowing abortion in these circumstances seems the obvious and kind thing to do, it is nevertheless victimising the unborn child and forcing it to pay the price for a serious act not of its doing. One possibility for a mother in this situation is for the child to be given up for adoption soon after birth.

However difficult the issues of rape and incest are, we need to return to the big picture. Making a general rule based on exceptional examples is not a good policy. As the maxim goes, 'hard cases make bad law'. Exceptional evils like rape and incest have been used to justify huge numbers of abortions, most of which are for reasons of social convenience. Life is complex and often difficult, but the unborn need protection and our society has abandoned them. We have allowed the termination of millions of unborn children. Those concerned with the value of human life must speak out to protect these most vulnerable members of our society.

The Church and Abortion

The question of how the church deals with the issue of abortion, and pastors those involved, requires careful thought. Some pro-choice advocates say that, as Christians appear to be against abortion, they are therefore against those women who decide to have an abortion.

Clearly Christians value all human life, since all human beings are created in the image of God. They seek to protect the unborn who cannot protect themselves. But there should be great compassion for women who are expecting a child and feel, for whatever reason, that they do not want to continue with the pregnancy. There is a recognition that there are many women who find themselves in very difficult situations, and the church should support them. In saying that abortion is wrong, Christians are not opposing women but are wanting to look after the unborn. The unborn should not be the ones to pay the price for decisions that adults make, which some may later regret.

Christians are not being self-righteous when they speak out against abortion. At the very heart of the Christian faith is the belief that we are all 'sinners'. Christians do not see themselves any differently from anyone else. The Christian gospel is about forgiveness, and anyone who has had an abortion should know that there is no deed beyond the scope of God's love and capacity to forgive. The church should welcome and care for women who have had terminations while supporting women who decide to continue with their pregnancy, even if having the child will prove burdensome.

The terms 'pro-choice' and 'pro-life' can muddy the waters. Because Christians value life, they want to encourage women who find themselves pregnant to make the choice to value this life and carry it to term, because no child is an 'accident'. All life is given by God and we have a moral obligation to protect it.

Notes

[17] https://www.nhs.uk/conditions/abortion/

[18] http://www.johnstonsarchive.net/policy/abortion/ab-unitedkingdom.html

[19] https://www.gov.uk/government/statistics/abortion-statistics-for-england-and-wales-2017

[20] *Independent*, Thursday 13 June, 2019.

[21] *Abortion*, Christian Legal Centre, Christian Concern, p.8.

[22] Ibid., p. 10.

[23] Christian Institute briefing.

[24] B Rooney and B C Calhoun, Journal of American Physicians and Surgeons, 2003, pp. 46-49.

[25] https://www.nhs.uk/conditions/abortion/risks/

[26] CBR UK is a campaign group whose purpose is to educate society as to the humanity of an unborn child and the reality of abortion. They do not condemn people who have had abortions.

[27] Valerie Tarico, Free Inquiry, Vol.36, No 5, August 2016.

[28] John Feinberg, Paul Feinberg, Ethics for a Brave New World, p. 90.

[29] J Carl Laney, in Vital Contemporary Issues, p. 41.

[30] Nancy Pearcey, *Love Thy Body*, p. 49.

[31] Cynthia Isabell, The Torch – *A Light in Dark Places*, 2 August 2016. Before the placenta develops the embryo is not separated in this way, though it is genetically distinct from her and not comprised of her cells.

Chapter 6

The Redefinition of Marriage and the Destruction of the Family

Another issue where there are discords in our society is marriage and the family. Christians, as well as some other religious groups, have had a very high view of marriage. The same is true of those who describe themselves as social conservatives. Marriage and the family have been a foundational part of society across the globe for thousands of years. Progressive liberal morality has negated the centrality of the family and the importance of marriage, while marriage itself has been redefined. This has not happened suddenly or in giant steps but rather, gradually and with subtle shifts. However, these institutions are now under greater threat than at any point in our lifetime.

An example of this was a BBC programme, Question Time, that was broadcast on 15 June 2012. The issue being discussed was welfare reform. Representing the Labour Party on the panel was Emily Thornberry, a former barrister turned politician, and Shadow Attorney General.[32] Also on the panel was the journalist Peter Hitchens, a Christian, and brother of the late atheist thinker, Christopher. A member of the audience asked a question about welfare and as part of his reply, Hitchens argued that a significant problem in society was the destruction of the 'married family' and the deliberate subsidising of fatherless families. Thornberry, who herself comes from a single-parent family, verbally assaulted Hitchens, claiming that he was ridiculing all those brave women who work hard to bring up their children on their own. The strength of her invective masked the fact that Hitchens had said no such thing. However, this debate illustrates the fact that as soon as Christians (or indeed any other moral conservatives) express their traditional views on marriage and the family, they are immediately denounced as being bigoted and phobic about any non-traditional family arrangement.

This attitude towards traditional family values and those who hold to them is growing. These views have given rise to a new term, 'woke culture'. In the words of Douglas Murray, woke culture is 'political correctness after a course of steroids. Its followers spend their lives punishing any wrong-think committed, which can include thinking something everyone thought until yesterday. And includes saying things that are true'.[33] In the same article he states, 'The main inspirations for the 'wokerati' are anything to do with relations between the sexes, race, LGBT issues, and the last of these (Trans) in particular. In each case a legitimate rights debate is weaponised into a culture war'.

The criticisms faced by Christians and other social conservatives are unjust and false. However, in order to address them in a rational manner, we need to work through the issues in stages.

The Importance of Marriage and Family

We need to begin by underlining just how significant is the institution of marriage and how important is the family. In dealing with marriage we can go back to Genesis to grasp the biblical view.

The creation stories of Genesis 1 and 2 show us different facets of the same reality. In Genesis 1:27 we read that, 'God made mankind in His own image, male and female he created them'. Men and woman were made equal, equally bearing the image of God. Chapter 2 tells us why female had to be created as well as male: Genesis 2:18 states, 'It is not good for the man to be alone'. Humans are social creatures; we need company. This is true in a general sense, but here God expresses it in a special sense, though this verse does not invalidate singleness as a positive lifestyle. Genesis is pointing out that men and women need each other; there is a complementarity between them, and the survival of the human race depends on their being together in relationship. Further amplification is found in verse 20 where we read, 'for Adam no suitable helper was found'. God had created lots of animals, but they were inferior to human beings and of a different order, so they could not add to the man's life in any ultimately meaningful way.

The term 'helper' used in this passage does not imply any inferiority, or that the woman is weaker, or there for the man's convenience. In fact, the term can sometimes refer to military aid or even to divine help.[34]

But neither does the word mean that the helper is stronger than the man. The point being made here is that the man is inadequate by himself as a solitary being and he needs someone else to share life with. The woman is a suitable partner, she is a perfect fit, the appropriate person to share life with. This fitness can be found in every way, including sexually.

In verses 21 and 22 Adam was put into a deep sleep, a rib was taken from him and Eve was created. It may be that poetic language is being used here, but this does not detract from the clarity of the meaning. With the creation of Eve, the man was complete, and the writer is informing us that this is how the world ought to be. These are the Creator's instructions.

Two important points should be emphasised. First, God created only two genders and His image is invested in only two genders. Whatever our culture would try to tell us, this is a binary creation in line with all the animals having their respective partners. Secondly, man is perfectly complemented by woman and that is the union that God had in mind from the beginning.

This narrative is followed up by the comment in verse 24 that a man, 'leaves his father and mother ... and they become one flesh'. The inference here is that sexual union and the profound relationship that accompanies it is something to be experienced between a man and a woman. It is part of their unique compatibility. It is a union and a relationship they commit themselves to in an exclusive way and to which they give priority, even to the point of a man cutting some of his family ties so he can commit exclusively to the woman.

At this point we need to refer back to Genesis 1:28 to note something else. Having made male and female and invested His image in them, God tells them, 'Be fruitful and increase in number'. This is very significant and a hugely important piece of theology. One of the primary reasons, perhaps the most important reason, for sex is procreation. Of course, sex is not only for this. The beautiful poetry of the Song of Songs assures us that the sexual union is for pleasure and the enhancement of a relationship. It is something to be celebrated as a good in and of itself. Nevertheless, at the heart of the sexual act is the important issue of procreation. This not only guarantees the survival of the human race, it is also an expression of the image of God in us, because through sexual union we too become creators.

There are many couples who go through the pain of childlessness which causes very real distress. In a broken world such realities are sadly present and a reminder of the need for our world and everyone in it to be redeemed. Nevertheless, this picture of man and woman in sexual union to produce successive generations is an important one. Our culture has gone the opposite way. It has reduced sexuality to a recreational activity, something that is often devoid of commitment, emotion and loyalty. In civil law, the boundaries have been destroyed so that it is not confined to the divinely given parameters of one man and one woman in a monogamous and binding relationship for life.

A Christian View of Marriage

When we leave the creation narratives of Genesis and study the rest of Scripture, it is clear that the Bible holds marriage in very high esteem. The prophet Malachi described marriage as a covenant between a man and a woman (Mal. 2:14). In other words, marriage is a solemn agreement that a couple make, in which they commit to be faithful to each other throughout their lives. Marriage ceremonies were and are conducted publicly so that family and community can hold the couple accountable to their vows. But Scripture also makes it clear that God joins a couple together (Matt. 19:6), because marriage is His design for the world, not just for Christians or Jews. That is why Jesus stated in Matthew 19:4-5 that marriage existed 'at the beginning'.

The esteem in which the Bible holds marriage is further emphasised by the fact that marriage is pictured alongside the relationship of Christ and His church (Eph. 5:31-32). Both are to be highly treasured and respected. The Bible also deals with any threats to marriage. As we noted in chapter 4, God told His people, 'You shall not commit adultery' (Exod. 20:14). As one of the Ten Commandments, this was to form part of the bedrock of Jewish ethics. The same command is also mentioned numerous times in the New Testament (Matt. 15:19; Luke 18:20; Rom. 2:22; Jas 2:11). Adultery is wrong precisely because the intruder in an adulterous relationship comes in between the 'one flesh' of the marriage bond. The fact that adultery is so damaging, painful and undermining demonstrates what a betrayal of trust it is. It is more than just a sexual act; it corrodes what ought to be a solid and loving relationship. It is so serious that the Jews were commanded that they should not even think about it (Exod. 20:17). Moreover, Jesus said that if a man were to even look at a woman lustfully, he would be committing adultery in his heart (Matt. 5:27-28).

It must be borne in mind that Christians throughout the centuries have had an unwavering commitment to marriage, since they have understood the great weight that Scripture gives to it. Indeed, as Brian Hadley points out, the Christian commitment to marriage is why Christianity has become 'the principal target of "sexual rights" activists, because it tells people who engage in intimate behaviours outside real marriage that such behaviours are wrong'.[35]

Marriage is so important in Scripture that there are clear boundaries placed around it. For example, in Leviticus 18:6-18, incest was strictly prohibited. Likewise, there were punishments for people who had sex before marriage (Exod. 22:16-17). Women were commanded to remain virgins until their marriage (Deut. 22:13-21), demonstrating that sexual activity was clearly something for the marriage relationship alone.

The Bible is equally clear and unequivocal that marriage, and indeed all sexual expression, is to be between a man and a woman. There are several passages where homosexuality is clearly prohibited. In Leviticus 18:22 and 20:13 homosexual relationships are strongly condemned. Genesis 19 tells the story of the destruction of Sodom and Gomorrah. They were destroyed for their wickedness and among their many sins was that of homosexual practice. The strength of the biblical prohibition against homosexual practice is clarified in Romans 1 where Paul talks about how human culture has fallen; one of the signs of the distortion which the Fall produces is the giving up of natural relationships for unnatural ones (Rom. 1:26-27).

Some Christians have tried to interpret these and other passages to suggest that they refer only to excessive practices such as pederasty (that is, sex between a man and a boy) and homosexual rape, and consequently should not be taken as a condemnation of a stable and loving homosexual relationship. However, the clarity of the overall sweep of Scripture makes such exegesis implausible. Moreover, homosexual relationships in the Bible are always seen in a negative light, in complete contrast to its celebration of heterosexual relationships. As Kevin DeYoung states, 'There is no positive case for homosexual practice in the Bible and no historical background that will allow us to set aside what has been the plain reading of Scripture for nearly twenty centuries.'[36]

We should be careful not to single out homosexual practice as sin and disregard others, because all sin is wrong. Moreover, we cannot fall back on the argument that sees a homosexual attraction as a specific or unique effect of the Fall any more than other evidence of our fallenness. The truth is that we are all fallen people, and the effects of the Fall not only impact all of us but taint every facet of our being. As humans, sin affects our will (John 8:34), our minds (Genesis 6:5), our emotions (Romans 1:24), our speech (2 Timothy 3:3) and our behaviour (Galatians 5:19). The Fall also affects us in the sexual arena. Heterosexual males have a fallen human nature and therefore their sexuality is also fallen, as is the case with their same-sex attracted friends. If we are Christians, holiness should be our goal; that applies to homosexuals and heterosexuals alike – there is no difference. If someone who is same-sex attracted begins to follow Jesus, their primary goal is not to become heterosexual, rather it is to be holy. As Ed Shaw rightly points out, if we equate godliness with heterosexuality, then no one will be able to grasp how a same-sex attracted Christian can live a godly life.[37] God's plan for the world does not include same-sex relationships, but neither does it include many of the activities that heterosexuals are guilty of.

Looking at the Threats

Having looked at God's pattern for marriage and the family, we now need to focus on the many ways in which the permissive values of our society encroach on this pattern. Doing so, potentially puts us in the firing line for the kind of angry response mentioned at the start of this chapter. However, traditional marriage and the family are such fundamental building blocks in society that they must be defended.

Why Marry?

The first threat is one in which the importance of marriage is simply negated by our culture at large. Many people believe in marriage and see it as important and something to be treasured. They might do this because of a religious conviction, but equally, people of no religious conviction view the institution of marriage as important and commit to it. However, a significant number of people have a very casual and even cynical attitude towards marriage and demonstrate it by their actions. For example, some see marriage as an outdated institution and would much rather cohabit if they are in relationship with someone. For others, for example radical feminists, it is a 'sell-out' that keeps women in subjugation. The widespread practice of casual sex and our 'hook up' culture is further evidence of the lack of respect for marriage. The latter demonstrates that some people want the physical benefits of a sexual relationship without the commitment that marriage requires. The recent opening of civil partnerships to heterosexual couples may prove to be a further erosion of the institution of marriage.

The lifestyle which these attitudes promote has inevitably led to a significant rise in the number of single parent families. The increase in the number of divorces until recently (this has now levelled off) has also been an important contributory factor. While there are instances when separation and divorce may, from the point of view of one party, be justified, the rise in divorce reflects a lack of commitment to marriage. Many couples have not deemed their marriage important enough to fight for it, and divorce, along with lone parenting, has been the outcome.

Many single parents behave sacrificially – women and also men who are deeply committed to their children – and have worked hard to give them a loving and stable home. Nevertheless, the data clearly demonstrates that, viewed across society as a whole, children who grow up in a stable family environment where their parents are married, obtain significant benefits.[38] For example, children who live with their own two married parents have significantly higher educational achievement and are much more likely to enjoy a better economic standard in their adult lives. Children who live with their own two married parents have better emotional and physical health and are less likely to commit crime or to engage with alcohol or substance abuse. The effects of single-parent families may have an even greater impact on boys than on girls. There is an increasing body of research that demonstrates that boys develop differently and have distinct social, domestic and educational needs.[39] They relate to their fathers and their mothers quite differently and each relationship meets distinct emotional and developmental needs.

These are generalities and there are many children from single parent families who have done well, feel secure and are happy. Nevertheless, the overall data should not be ignored if we value the nation's children.

Divorce Made Easy

Divorce has been around for a long time, though it was made significantly easier by the Divorce Law Reform Act of 1969, and our law allows for it under a variety of circumstances. However, there is increasing pressure to liberalise the law and therefore make divorce easier to obtain. Legislation for so-called 'no-fault divorce' is currently being proposed.

Under existing UK law, divorce is permitted if it is believed that the marriage has broken down irretrievably. There are five grounds for granting divorce on this basis. They include living apart, desertion and adultery. However, the proposed new legislation would remove the five grounds thereby making the route to divorce much quicker and easier. The time that it takes to get a divorce could drop to six months, increasing the incentive to divorce and reducing the likelihood of a reconciliation. Those wanting to escape from their marriage may be eager for such legislation to go through, but given the existing prevalence of divorce, with some 100,000 being granted in 2017, it is clear that this legislation is detrimental to society.[40] Divorce causes great damage to spouses as well as children and the consequences of a 'divorce made easy' policy would be likely to greatly increase the pain. Moreover, the removal of the grounds for divorce changes the nature of marriage for those entering into it from that of a covenant with mutual obligations to that of a temporary arrangement that can be terminated at will by either party without a reason. (The correct name for the proposal should therefore be 'no reason divorce' rather than 'no fault divorce' and some have, perhaps inappropriately, therefore likened it to divorce under Sharia law.)

The Redefinition of Marriage

A further significant threat to marriage and the family is the redefinition of marriage which allows for same-sex couples to get married. This is a sensitive issue, as the LGBT community may denounce people as 'homophobic' if they do not warmly endorse what are called 'LGBT+

rights'. Christians should condemn any harassment, bullying or ridiculing of people who are same-sex attracted. Nor would many Christians want to roll back the clock to a time prior to 1967 (when homosexuality was decriminalised). That said, the implications of lifestyle choices for society still need to be subject to proper scrutiny.

Proponents celebrate same-sex relationships and strive to not only normalise their practice but also resist any attempt to discuss the legitimate questions they raise. A homosexual lifestyle potentially carries health risks and the same can be said of casual heterosexual relationships. Nevertheless, the evidence suggests the risks are greater within the homosexual community.[41] The risk of infection is such that the blood transfusion service in the UK does not accept donations of blood from men or women who have had recent sexual relationships with male homosexuals.[42] This data is rarely highlighted, for as Satinover comments, 'In spite of clear evidence that homosexual standards are strikingly different from the heterosexual norm, the general public impression has been created that gays are little different from straights.'[43]

Are Traditional and Same-Sex Marriage Equivalent?

The issue of so-called 'equal marriage' needs to be reflected on, because with the legal definition of marriage now broadened to include same-sex marriage, the nature of traditional marriage has been brought into question. What needs to be questioned is whether same-sex marriage can be considered the equivalent of heterosexual marriage. This is not in any way to ignore the love and commitment that might exist between two men or between two women. Rather, it is to raise the issue of whether these relationships can be essentially the same as that of a heterosexual marriage. A fundamental difference is that procreation is only possible through heterosexual relationships and therefore in a biological sense the two cannot be equated. Some will point out that people beyond childbearing age marry, but this is does not detract from the essential biological complementarity of the relationship. Historically, the use of the term 'marriage' has always been taken to mean a union between a man and a woman. This is at least partly because people perceived that marriage is founded upon the potential for procreation. In that sense, while the State can allow certain liberties and rights for same-sex couples, if they define their union as 'marriage' then the State is overturning thousands of years of human history and culture. If same-sex marriage and heterosexual marriage are not equivalent, it begs the bigger question as to whether both types of marriage are equally beneficial for society.

What about the Children?

If a government legalises same-sex marriage and purports to make it the equivalent of traditional marriage, this opens up the possibility of children becoming part of the equation. In the UK as in other countries this is already the case, but the debate is still live in many countries around the world.

A same-sex couple is not able to have children by natural means. However, they could use an external parent to produce a child, or they could adopt. Some advocates argue that it is better for children to live with loving same-sex parents than it is to live with heterosexual parents who are not loving. However, this does not answer the question, because both could be damaging and therefore both could be wrong. The comparison is therefore not a good or helpful one. Moreover, as John Scriven rightly states, this issue, 'should not be addressed from the perspective of alleged discrimination against those seeking to adopt. Rather, the debate should be about the public good, focusing on the interests of the child, rather than the so-called human rights of prospective same-sex parents'.[44] This assessment is surely correct; after all, the prospective parents are able to make choices about their lifestyles, whereas the children, who are by definition vulnerable, have no choice in the matter.

Evidence of the effects of same-sex parenting is not widely known. However, there is research spanning decades that does suggest the importance of children growing up in a home that is stable, with both a father and mother.[45] This should surely not surprise us, because humans have been designed to live in just such an environment.

Given the differences between men and women, children benefit from the support, love and education of being raised by both a father and a mother. In the light of the security that this provides for a child, we should be hesitant to undermine these benefits for the sake of political correctness. Moreover, as the whole field of social sciences is subject to significant cultural pressure, we need to think through this issue very carefully and in a dispassionate way. Indeed, as Walter Schumm points out in his definitive study of over 400 research papers on the outcomes of same-sex parenting, 'There do appear to be significant and substantial differences between same-sex and heterosexual parents and in long-term outcomes for their children, contrary to many, many allegations by numerous social scientists over the decades'.[46] Children benefit from the balance of having both a father figure and a mother figure. Moreover, marriage is a unique relationship which has been the foundation stone for the family, which is in turn the basic unit of society. Any attempt to jeopardise this institution has potentially serious social consequences.

Many have argued that same-sex marriage is about love, and that the government, as well as society at large, have no right to deny same-sex couples the right to get married for, after all, love trumps all else. However, good governance is about making judgment calls in relation to what is good for society. There is a prohibition on two siblings marrying and also on an adult marrying a child. Both of these are considered wrong and the issue of love does not negate this.[47]

Same-sex marriage is already permitted in many countries including the UK, but the debate must surely continue as to whether this is good for our society, not least as a safeguard against future changes. Same-sex couples should be protected, like any other people, against unlawful behaviour. However, that does not mean that society should be compelled to approve same-sex relationships and view them in the same way that it does a heterosexual relationship. There must be the openness in a free and democratic society to have frank and honest discussions about these issues without the fear of being called 'homophobic'. Christians have raised objections in this area not because they harbour hatred for the LGBT community. On the contrary, the desire of Christians is to love their neighbour, and that injunction includes everyone. They are equally concerned for society and the impact that social policy has on families and children, including through education. It is out of this concern for the common good of society that they want to protect and promote traditional understanding of marriage because they genuinely believe in its value.

Government Interference

A threat to marriage and the family is when government feels the need to interfere in family life and to usurp the responsibilities that normally would lie with parents. There are two examples of this that immediately come to mind. October 3rd 2019 was a significant day for families in Scotland because on that day the smacking ban came into law. This legislation effectively criminalised parents who would use smacking as a form of chastisement. It means that, subject to conditions (which 'pro-choice' activists would like to dispense with) you can legally kill your child while he or she is in the womb but cannot smack him or her once they are born.

Many parents do not use smacking as a form of correction. However, the language used in the debate was highly emotive. Campaigners talked about parents 'assaulting' their children, of inflicting 'harm' or simply 'hitting' them, when in fact the action which they were condemning was a proportionate use of force administered in a loving context. Parents will understand the difference. The worrying thing about this debate, however, was not so much the criminalisation of parents but rather, the government's desire to take decision making away from parents and to adjudicate for themselves what constitutes good parenting.

The same kind of insidious policy was demonstrated, once again in Scotland, by the abortive 'Named Person Scheme'. This very controversial piece of legislation was debated by the Scottish Parliament. According to this scheme, every child in Scotland was to be given a 'named person', who would be a State official tasked with the responsibility of looking after its wellbeing. The legislation required the named person to record and share confidential information about the child and its parents.

What the Scottish Government was trying to do was sideline parents and their rights in favour of what would amount to a kind of government-funded surveillance network. Though the Scottish Government defended itself against such a charge, the fundamental question needed to be asked, 'Who cares for Scotland's children more, Scottish parents or the government'? The answer is obvious. It is at the heart of a parent's job to care for their children; the attempt to usurp parental responsibility was an existential threat to the sanctity of family life. The scheme failed after lengthy legal action, as it was found to be in breach of the right to a private family life under the European Convention on Human Rights.[48] However, the very fact that a government could consider such legislation should be worrying. As Samuel Burgess rightly notes, 'If the reach of government actively becomes over-extended, it can radically shape a society according to its own vision; it ceases to govern and assumes an oppressive role'.[49] Usurping the rightful responsibility of parents is just such an example of over-extended governance.

Notes

[32] https://www.bbc.co.uk/news/av/uk-politics-18456466/peter-hitchens-phoney-outrage-over-welfare-reform

[33] https://www.dailymail.co.uk/debate/article-7833715/DOUGLAS-MURRAY-Good-riddance-2019-year-politically-correct-woke-police.html?ito

[34] Gordon J Wenham, *Genesis 1-15*, WBC, p.68.

[35] Lynda Rose (ed.), *What are They Teaching the Children?* p. 126.

[36] Kevin DeYoung, *What Does the Bible Really Teach about Homosexuality?* p. 87.

[37] Ed Shaw, *The Plausibility Problem*, p. 97

[38] Wayne Grudem, *Christian Ethics,* p. 739.

[39] Michael Nazir-Ali, *Faith, Freedom and the Future*, p. 127.

[40] https://www.christian.org.uk/campaign/no-fault-divorce/

[41] AM Johnson, K Wellings, *Sexual Attitudes and Lifestyles*, p. 213. See also Jeffrey Satinover, *Homosexuality and the Politics of Truth*, p. 54.

[42] Scottish National Blood Transfusion Service web site, (https://www.scotblood.co.uk/giving-blood/can-i-give-blood/)

[43] Jeffrey Satinover, *Homosexuality and the Politics of Truth*, p. 52.

[44] John Scriven, *Belief and the Nation*, p. 323.

[45] John Scriven, *Belief and the Nation*, p. 322.

[46] Walter R. Schumm, *Same Sex Parenting Research*, p. 227.

[47] Of course, there is no way of knowing how much longer these relationships will be considered to be wrong.

[48] https://www.christian.org.uk/campaign/named-person/

[49] Samuel Burgess, *The Moral Case for Conservatism*, p. 71.

Chapter 7

Transgender Culture

We now come to the third of the issues that we want to address, which relates to transgender people and the 'trans' culture. The idea of someone 'changing their sex' is not in itself new and neither are phenomena such as cross-dressing. However, the whole 'trans issue' has grown exponentially in the past decade and has begun to be a regular feature within the mainstream media. Indeed, in the words of social commentator Douglas Murray, 'Trans has become something close to a dogma in record time'.[50]

Such is the complexity of this issue that it is helpful to break it down into its component parts so that it can be clearly understood.

Gender Dysphoria

At the heart of this debate is a recognised medical condition known as gender dysphoria. The NHS defines this as 'a condition where a person experiences discomfort or distress because there's a mismatch between their biological sex and gender identity'.[51] To put this more simply, it is where someone who is, for example, biologically male, does not feel male but rather, female. These feelings can be so strong that it causes significant distress to the individual and promotes a longing in them to become or to be recognised as a member of the opposite sex.

There can be little doubt that the anxiety and distress that a person suffering from gender dysphoria feels is real.[52] There needs to be compassion for sufferers, though compassion alone is not enough; thought needs to be given to the best way of caring for people with this condition. Unfortunately, the cultural storm that has surrounded this issue has made it very difficult to speak rationally on the subject without incurring the hostility of the 'trans' community. Indeed, the very term gender dysphoria appears to be highly politicised. Previously it was referred to as gender identity disorder, but this term was thought to imply that the sufferer was out of kilter with what was normal. The new name, gender dysphoria, focuses more on the distress the person feels as opposed to the nature of the condition itself.

Within the UK, the issue of gender dysphoria has been debated extensively by clinicians and Parliament. The result of the political discussions was the Gender Recognition Act of 2004. This Act gave permission for a person to change their sex on condition that they fulfilled a list of criteria. These are as follows:

1. Have a medical diagnosis of gender dysphoria.
2. Obtain a report from a medical professional detailing any medical treatment.
3. Prove they have lived for at least two years in their acquired gender.
4. Make a statutory declaration that they intend to live in their acquired gender until death.
5. If married, have the consent of their spouse.
6. Pay a fee of £140 (the fee can be removed on proof of low income).
7. Submit this document to a panel which the applicant does not meet in person.

Once they have gone through this process and the conditions have been met, they receive a Gender Recognition Certificate and their birth certificate is also changed.

The Gender Recognition Act has not settled the issue in law, since there are people and pressure groups who think the process is still too cumbersome and lengthy. Politicians from different parties have also brought this Act into question. For example, when Justine Greening served as Equalities Minister as a member of the government of Prime Minister Theresa May, she called for the simplification of the Act, stating that it needed to be 'demedicalised' and also streamlined, so that people could simply self-identify; for her, that would be a sufficient criterion for being able to change gender. As of March 2020, it appears that the Government may be reconsidering whether this change should be proceeded with. Significantly, a number of feminists have objected on the grounds that it devalues their identity as women.

A Growing Storm

The cumulative effect is that a cultural tsunami has been created which appears to be sweeping all before it. Examples of this abound. Joshua Sutcliffe was a maths teacher in a high school in Oxfordshire. In his class was a girl who was transitioning to become a boy. Under his tutelage she had improved academically, but during a group work session he 'misgendered' her. She complained to her parents who complained to the school and Mr Sutcliffe was then suspended for this offence. If this were not bad enough, when he appeared on the ITV's Good Morning programme along with Andrea Williams from Christian Concern, they were criticised and insulted by presenter Philip Schofield, who finished the interview by saying, 'back to 2017 and not medieval Britain'.[53] This intolerance is becoming increasingly evident in the mainstream media.

Another person to be affected by the cultural maelstrom is leading feminist Germaine Greer. She not only withdrew from a speaking engagement at Cardiff University because of the reaction to the announcement of her coming, but she also faced the ignominy of an honorary doctorate being denied her from her own college, Newnham College, University of Cambridge. Her offence was to claim that transgender women were not real women.[54] This is of course, from a biological perspective, a statement of scientific fact, but in the atmosphere of this debate, rationality takes a backseat.

Universities on the other side of the Atlantic have also felt the pressure. One study by Lisa Littman suggested that gender dysphoria occurring around the time of puberty could be triggered by peer pressure and online influences. The report was published in the peer-reviewed journal PLOS ONE, but then removed by Brown University after protests.[55]

The challenge that this presents is serious. Popular culture and the media are so full of the 'trans conversation' that young people are inevitably going to be influenced by it.

Since the whole issue is so prevalent in our culture, it is not hard to imagine how young people who are questioning their identity might consider the possibility of transitioning. As Michele Moore rightly comments, 'The growing number of children identifying as transgender occurs against a backdrop of the media, the internet, medicine, education, social policy and politics, including trans activism. These interconnected influences provide the background to children's everyday lives and currently combine to popularise and make gender transitioning socially acceptable'.[56]

Dealing with Definitions

At this point something needs to be said about definitions. The term sex is a biological one. A person is either male or female depending on their physical sexual apparatus and their chromosomes (XX for male and XY for female). The term gender can be used interchangeably with sex but is a reference to the social and cultural differences between male and female. The 'trans' lobby attempts to pull these words apart, claiming that the term gender is only a cultural expression and that your gender does not need to correlate with your sex.

There is also a very rare condition that is referred to as intersex.[57] This is where a person is born with 'mixed-up' sex organs, hormone levels and an unusual configuration of chromosomes. While the term intersex is often included in the acronym LGBTI, it is in fact a completely different thing. The confusion that exists here is at a biological and physiological level and not just something in the mind.

Next there is a collection of terms such as transgender, genderqueer and gender dysphoria which describe a person who does not feel as if they fit into the biological sex of their body. Then there are said to be people who are cisgender, that is, people whose body and mind agree on what gender they are. These people are assumed to need a label like cisgender since they cannot, for reasons of political correctness, be referred to as 'normal'. Two more expressions worth noting are non-binary and gender-fluid. The former refers to people who are not simply male or female but rather, claim to represent multiple variations of gender. The latter refers to people who change their gender at will, depending on circumstances.

The presence of these terms demonstrates the widening nature of this debate. Indeed, a whole new vocabulary has been created as people have tried to outdo each other in identifying different forms of gender. When the Scottish Government brought out its anti-sectarian legislation in 2012, it declared that there were five genders. When the Children's Commissioner investigated the issue, he raised the number of claimed genders to 20. Not to be outdone, Facebook then indicated it believed there were 71 genders. More recently the BBC, always at the forefront of political correctness, declared there to be 100 genders.[58] All this leaves the question as to when this will stop.[59]

Reading the Culture

The growth of this debate leads us into the question, 'How does society at large view the whole issue of transgenderism?' One academic and writer who has made a significant contribution to this issue is Mark Yarhouse, who is the Chair in Psychology at Wheaton College in Illinois. Yarhouse claims helpfully that there are several lenses through which people view this issue:[60]

• Integrity framework: Firstly, there is the integrity framework where people view maleness and femaleness as essential to personhood. They are sacred categories that cannot be changed and should be accepted as such.

• Disability framework: Then there is the disability framework. This is viewing the issue through the lens of a fallen world. In a fallen world, things are not as they are meant to be and we should expect to see things that are real and present, but which we would not endorse or desire. Gender confusion is one of them.

• Diversity framework: Finally, there is the diversity framework where people see diversity as something to be applauded. For activists, transgender people should be celebrated as a normal part of life. In the same way that we might like living in a city where you can eat out in a Chinese, Italian or Indian restaurant, people also revel in the variety of gender forms. In this framework the distinctions between sex and gender are blurred.

Christians would tend to view the transgender issue through the integrity and disability frameworks. We believe that God made us male and female (Gen. 1:27) and that these are categories that exist in the creation order and which we have a duty to uphold. However, we recognise that our world is fallen and so we are not surprised when we see phenomena like gender dysphoria in our world. By way of contrast, Yarhouse argues that Western culture primarily views the present situation through the diversity framework. Critics of this position find themselves being accused of transphobia.

What Causes Gender Dysphoria?

The answer to this question is not straightforward, not least because there is still much research to be done on the issue. Even knowing how many suffer from gender dysphoria is difficult, as data can also be influenced by political concerns. However, at a rough estimate, we could claim that 1 in 10,000 men and 1 in 30,000 women will suffer from gender dysphoria.[61]

One theory that has gained some currency is referred to as the brain-sex theory. According to this thinking, in the same way that your body decided what sex it will be, so your brain also decides what gender it will be. Sometimes the two match and sometimes they do not match. The brain-sex theory has its supporters, and one of the reasons for this is that it purports to suggest a natural process by which people become transgender. However, there is a lack of evidence-based research supporting brain-sex theory, so those who hold to it can only do so tentatively.

At the heart of the debate on causation is the question whether transgenderism is the product of nurture or nature. That is, do people develop trans impulses as a result of a natural process (namely, they were born that way), or have they developed as a result of external circumstances? Once again, the evidence is as yet incomplete. Given the fallenness of our world, it is possible that some people are born with gender confusion; however, culture must also play an important role. The recent spike in people enquiring about transitioning must owe something to the very high profile which transgender issues have been given in the media and broader culture.

Approaches to Treatment

What kind of treatment is appropriate for people presenting with gender dysphoria? When a person is suffering from gender dysphoria, should their body be altered to conform to their gender identity, or should they be given psychological treatment or counselling aimed at reconciling their identity and biology? In other words, is gender dysphoria a problem of the body or the mind?

The rational, as well as the theological, answer would be that gender dysphoria is an issue of the mind and should be treated as such. It might help to compare gender dysphoria with another disorder, anorexia nervosa. In both cases the sufferer does not like his or her body, is distressed and preoccupied by it and wishes to change. However, if an underweight person with anorexia presented to a clinician stating that they were fat, a medical team would not acquiesce to the patient's self-image and fit a gastric band but rather, treat it as a disorder of the mind. To deal with the transgender issue by denying its psychological component is both short-sighted and potentially dangerous. Moreover, it defies rationality. Even if a man with gender dysphoria had surgery to become a woman, every cell in his body and every strand of DNA would still be male. A change of physical appearance and lifestyle does not negate the reality of biology.

Treatment for Children

One method of treating children who present with gender dysphoria could be described as a watchful, waiting approach. That is no bad thing as it involves patient observation rather than rushing in to try to treat the syndrome. Many children grow out of a desire to 'be the other sex', so if the clinicians (and parents) are patient, the problem may resolve itself in time.

If this does not happen, another form of treatment is to intervene to decrease cross-gender identification. This treatment treats the gender dysphoria as an issue of the mind rather than the body and works for reconciliation between body and mind. The Portman Clinic reports significant success with this method, with as many as 80% finding resolution.[62] If most children will grow out of transgender feelings and if intervention can lead to an 80% success rate, this should guide our attitudes and methodology on the issue.

Another treatment is to facilitate the child to make a transition to their chosen sex. Surgery should be out of the question until the child reaches the age of 18 and other preconditions are met. However, the child may be permitted to dress in a manner appropriate to their chosen gender and assume the role of that gender. One aspect of this treatment can be the use of puberty suppression drugs (puberty blockers). The purpose is to delay the onset of puberty to give the child more time to work out what gender they want to be. Apart from whether it is right in principle to disturb the course of nature in stopping growth, and also whether this is a legitimate use of medicine given that the child is not physically ill, Thomas and Saunders note that, 'There are additional concerns with puberty suppression about brain development, bone growth and subfertility, as well as the possibility that the dysphoria might naturally have abated at the age of 12 or 13, by the time the treatment would have commenced.[63] The potential seriousness of these side effects should cause us alarm.

Treatment for Adults

When it comes to adults, one approach is to identify and use the least invasive forms of treatment – not to 'cure' or find a permanent solution for the individual but rather, to alleviate some of the distress they feel about their bodies. Interestingly, many adults who identify as transgender and initiate some form of treatment eventually give up on the process, with the dropout rate being as high as 50%.[64] Trans activists argue that the dropout rate is due to the difficulty of the process and the attitude of people at large to the trans community. However, it is not clear that there is evidence for this.

Of those who undergo psychological treatment to help them accept their birth sex, the majority do not find resolution. Many of those suffering gender dysphoria have what are called 'comorbidities', which are other psychological or medical problems. The concern is that they may be persuaded that the answer to their problems is a change of gender when there are other conditions or issues that have not been resolved. Given the lack of data, it is difficult to state definitively how they go on to handle the situation, but it is probable that a proportion do so by getting involved in some form of intermittent transgender behaviour.

Not everyone who adopts a new gender will have hormone treatment or surgery. No doubt the invasive nature of these procedures is a contributory factor in this. Instead they opt for milder forms of behaviour such as cross-dressing. Some do go for surgery and of those who do many, but certainly not all, are satisfied with the outcome. We should, of course, also factor in the evidence that regret about surgery may not emerge until after some time. However, given that the clinical effect of surgery is to neuter the person by what is akin to mutilation resulting in only superficial characteristics of the chosen sex, concerns must be raised about whether the treatment is ethically justified. These concerns are highlighted by those who do not experience a good outcome and want to de-transition. However, for all, there are likely to be complexities. Those who suffer from gender dysphoria experience higher levels of suicidal behaviour and psychiatric morbidity than the general population. They are troubled people and the need for compassion is evident.

Should We be Concerned?

Given the complexities already mentioned, it should be clear that this is a significant issue and one that should cause us some concern – in six specific areas:

1. *The limits of self-identification*

The first concern relates to the limits of self-identification. If people in the trans community wish to 'de-medicalise' the process and remove science and expert opinion by allowing an individual to self-identify, there needs to be a discussion about the consequences since this would remove any objective safeguards.

The example of Adam Wheeler is a case in point.[65] He is a young, white male from the United States. However, he self-identifies as a middle-aged female from the Philippines. In other words, his self-identification ignores the physical reality of his gender, age and nationality. Such is his desire to identify in this way, he even drives a tuk-tuk. The eccentric nature of this example underlines a serious issue. If self-identification is allowed to become the arbiter, where will it stop? For example, could a 40-year-old man begin to identify as a nine-year-old and request admission to a primary school? Or could a white male identify as a black person and then demand the benefits of a quota system that is aimed at assisting minority groups? While these examples might seem outlandish, they are no less logical than someone whose body, down to their every DNA strand, is male and yet wishes to be recognised by society at large as female. No amount of compassion for those who suffer from gender dysphoria should negate the valid concerns related to self-identification.

2. *The potential for child abuse*
A second concern is the real potential for what might be considered a form of child abuse. Children are children; maturation does not take place overnight but rather, comes as a result of a slow process. A major milestone in this process that leads to maturity is puberty. A child that has yet to go through puberty is simply too young to know exactly who they are in relation to their sexuality, not least because their full sexual development has not yet taken place. Neither is it uncommon for children to have lots of questions about themselves, many, if not all, of which will be resolved in time. Encouraging children to question their sexual identity at this vulnerable stage in their lives, and administering puberty blockers to delay their sexual maturing, is dangerous.

It is not hard to imagine how an over-zealous parent, with a particular worldview and life orientation, might affirm their child's self-questioning and even encourage their child to think about gender transition if he or she raises questions about their gender. The same pressure might come from teachers, social workers and peers, as well as from wider culture. That same child might be encouraged into accepting treatment at a stage in life when they are simply not equipped to make a reasoned decision about such a critical issue. The presence of charities such as Mermaids in primary schools is a cause for serious worry. Clinics such as the Tavistock Clinic have caused concern for the same reason, even to the point of eliciting protest from their own staff.[66] Administering hormone blockers to young children in order to 'buy time' is by its nature an invasive step too far, and one which comes close to being child abuse.

3. *When the 'trans train' leaves the station*
There is also a longer-term reason to be concerned about. This reason is powerfully portrayed in the Swedish documentary 'The Trans Train'. In this film two men tell their story of transitioning from being men into trans women. It is a very moving biopic and one which illustrates powerfully the regret that transgender people can experience once they have gone through the whole process and have transitioned into their chosen gender. The reality is that, depending on the surgery, once it is done there is usually no going back.[67]

The desire to change is genuine, as is the desire that others accept the change. However, the radical nature of what some have gone through cannot be overestimated, and they may later regret what they have done. As we have already noted, when people go through surgery, they do not actually become the opposite sex. Every cell in their body remains the same, carrying the same DNA (whether male or female) which they had before the treatment. As Paul McHugh, Johns Hopkins Professor of Psychiatry, comments, 'Transgender men do not become women, nor do transgender women become men. All become feminised men or masculinised women, counterfeits or impersonators of the sex with which they identify.'[68]

As the documentary demonstrates, once the 'trans train' has left the station there is no return. It is for this very reason that the Gender Recognition Act included some safeguards. Legal actions against those who encouraged and carried out the transition treatment are already beginning.

4. *Practical problems*

There are a number of practical problems that transitioning throws up. There is the use of public toilets and the fact that some people may be uncomfortable with a trans woman using female toilets or a trans man using male toilets. Likewise, female patients might be uncomfortable receiving treatment from a trans woman doctor. Such objections may be denounced as transphobic, but that response fails to engage seriously with the issue.

Then there are cases of male prisoners who transition and request to be placed in female prisons. A case in point is Karen White, a remand prisoner who entered the prison system as transgender, even though 'she' had not had gender reassignment surgery and was still legally a male. White was a convicted paedophile and had a history of violence against women. While in prison 'she' assaulted two other inmates. The Ministry of Justice has since apologised, but this account highlights the danger.

We should also bear in mind the potential for difficulties in the world of sport. If men transition to become women, should they be allowed to compete with women in sport and does their biology give them an unfair advantage? Laurel Hubbard from New Zealand, who began life as Gavin, competed as a male weightlifter before transitioning in her thirties. Competing as a woman at the 2019 Pacific Games, she won two gold medals and one silver in the heavyweight category. Women's groups have complained about the unfair advantage she has; the controversy is set to continue as Hubbard is qualified to compete as a woman in the 2020 Tokyo Olympics (as of March 2020, postponed to 2021).

5. *The lie of transphobia*

A fifth issue that is of concern is the way any debate gets closed down by politically correct critics. As soon as someone raises questions about transgender issues they can be fiercely denounced as being 'transphobic'.

There is an important difference between asking genuine questions about transgender culture and disliking or hating someone who is transgender. Christian faith demands that we love others, even those with whom we disagree and those who might hate us. It is a convenient lie to make the accusation of transphobia as freely as many protagonists do. It is the trans lobby which, in closing down debate, is intolerant and so often blind to reality and rationality.

6. *A low view of the body*

People suffering from gender dysphoria have a low view of their own bodies. Of course, many people are dissatisfied with their bodies for a variety of reasons. Some think they are too fat, others too pale and still others feel they are too thin. Body confidence has become a big issue. However, there is a point where the dislike that someone has for their own body becomes unhealthy. This will especially be the case if their body is otherwise healthy and fit for purpose.

Our bodies are a good and necessary thing; they are part of God's good work of creation. They are not there to be mutilated and damaged but rather, treasured and respected. Even people with no religious leanings and no concept of God as Creator, have a respect for their own and other people's bodies. If a perfectly healthy patient went to their doctor complaining that they didn't like their arm and wanted to have it removed, the doctor would be unlikely just to agree and encourage them to have surgery. Why then, when a man has a healthy body, do we assume it is normal and acceptable to remove the physical markers of his masculinity in order to allow him to feel more like a woman? Nancy Pearcey likens these transgender impulses to a form of 'self-hate', as the individual has a low regard for their own body.[69] She likens it to a black person who might try and pass as a white person; it denies the reality of who the person really is. We should have compassion for people who suffer in this way, but that does not mean that we should agree with their low assessment of their bodies.

A Biblical Perspective

Christians should approach the issue of gender dysphoria with compassion for those who suffer. There is wide recognition that this is a real condition that causes genuine distress. However, it is not compassionate to accept someone's self-identification or agree with their desire to transition. Responsible Christians express concern not just for the individual and their proper treatment, but also for the impact on society at large.

The Bible has much to say on the issue. In verse 27 of the first chapter of Genesis we are told that God made gender binary, that is, male and female. The image of God is equally seen in both masculinity and femininity and the biblical writer allows for no other categorisation. Jesus Himself repeated this assertion, recognising that there were two genders (Matt. 19:4-5).

The Psalmist also has a contribution to make to this discussion. In Psalm 139:13-16 he pictures a loving Creator God who actively constructs a child in its mother's womb. Verse 14 declares that each child is 'fearfully and wonderfully made'. Clearly that includes that person's sex and their biological sexual markers. The Psalmist also makes the remarkable claim (v. 16) that God has a purpose for every human being even before they begin to live out any of their days. The beauty of this passage is the way it expresses how we are valued as people, including our physical bodies. To deny what our physical bodies are telling us about ourselves is therefore not good. Indeed, as 1 Corinthians 13:6 reminds us, love rejoices in the truth. God has made us who we are, and we should accept that.

We live in a fallen world, and in such a world we should expect to find both pain and confusion. However, the work of the Cross deals not only with personal sin but also with the damage caused by the Fall. In Romans 8:22-23 Paul talks about the redemption of creation, which is our future hope. However, it is significant that he also mentions the renewing of our bodies. This is a hope that can be offered to everyone suffering from gender dysphoria that, in the future, in God's plan, they can be made whole.

The Church and Transgenderism

Given that the gospel is for all, and Christianity welcomes people irrespective of who they are and their background, it should be an aspiration in churches to reach out to the transgender community. For everyone, the offer of the gospel is accompanied by the possibility of transformation. Trans people are no exception when it comes to the healing that Christians believe that God can bring in all of our lives.

Churches should respond to people suffering from gender dysphoria with a welcome and a love that is unconditional. It does not matter what expression a person may have given to their dysphoria. They may simply be experiencing the feeling of distress that they are in the wrong body, or they may have been living in their chosen sex or have had surgery. Love does not mean that the church should accept a person's assessment that they are a different gender from their birth sex. Neither does it imply that the church is willing to acquiesce with the new liberal agenda. Indeed, as Owen Strachan warns, 'The church is not to pitch itself somewhere slightly below what we would call the "Ideal Spiritual Mark". In other words, we do not soften our spirituality to attract lost people'.[70] Nevertheless we must act with compassion, and the welcome we offer should express the love that God has for all people irrespective of their personal circumstances.

Secondly, the church should offer a sense of community for people with gender dysphoria. This is important because many sufferers already feel lonely and isolated and are longing for a sense of belonging. They may have already experienced rejection and derision from other people and even unfair and prejudicial treatment. The church has an opportunity to give people with gender dysphoria the sense of belonging which they may desperately need. It is that sense of community which will be of significant help in the person finding resolution. It will be a crucial part of their discipleship should they choose to follow Christ.

Thirdly, if someone with gender dysphoria does decide to take a step of faith and follow Jesus Christ, part of their discipleship will be to recognise their true given identity. When people begin their journey of faith as Christians, they come as they are, but they do not remain as they are, for true Christianity involves personal transformation. This will not be easy; neither (miracles apart) will it be an instant or even a quick process. Anyone who has had dealings with mental health issues will know that finding wholeness is an immense challenge. For many people suffering from gender dysphoria, the pathway towards acceptance of who they are will often be faltering, and they may have to live with the tension of being on a perpetual journey. Part of the role of the church is to facilitate and offer guidance and support for people as they experience whatever transformation faith can bring.

We need to recognise that this will be a difficult journey. An essential part of following Jesus Christ is a willingness to carry one's cross, no matter how painful. We will also need to teach (for this issue as well as for others) a robust theology of suffering. This is not just so that the individual does not feel isolated, but because every believer may well have to face suffering. In this we also have a role model who can be trusted even in these difficult and sensitive situations. As Andrew Walker reminds us, we have, 'a crucified Creator God who has the authority to tell us what to do, who has the wisdom to know what is best for us, and who has proved that he can be trusted to tell us what is best for us'.[71] Nevertheless, the journey of following Jesus and being true to the person that God made you to be, even at great cost, is one which the church should encourage Christians with gender dysphoria to take, even if they will at times stumble in the process.[72]

Fourthly, the church should always keep a redemptive future in mind (Rom. 8:22-24). The work of the Cross not only saves us for eternal life, it also provides the opportunity for healing which can begin now, and which will reach completion in the new creation. We know that full redemption will only reach completion in the world to come. In this one we continue, even as Christians, to live with the fallenness of our present experience. Redemption is in process and we should have this in mind as we care for people, whatever their challenges.

Notes

[50] Douglas Murray, The Madness of Crowds, p.186.

[51] https://www.nhs.uk/conditions/gender-dysphoria

[52] Of course, a person feeling the mismatch does not automatically mean that there is a mismatch in a strictly 'ontological' sense. However, dealing with how a person 'feels' rather than some physical reality is complex. We cannot deny the feeling, even though the feeling may not reflect reality.

[53] https://www.youtube.com/watch?v=_9_b49s-xVg

[54] https://www.youtube.com/watch?v=7B8Q6D4a6TM https://www.independent.co.uk/news/people/germaine-greer-will-not-give-cardiff-university-lecture-because-of-abuse-over-views-on-transgender-a6707236.html

[55] https://www.nbcnews.com/feature/nbc-out/brown-university-criticized-over-removal-transgender-study-n906741

[56] Michele Moore, Transgender Children and Young People, p.220.

[57] It should be stated that 'intersex' is not actually a single condition but an umbrella term for several conditions.

[58] https://www.youtube.com/watch?v=wandALGRoqU

[59] Yarhouse rightly states that in the debate we need to be able to distinguish between the political advocates of transgenderism, those living with the public persona and those suffering from gender dysphoria, otherwise we will miss those who genuinely need our care (Understanding Transgender Identities, pp. 120-121).

[60] Mark Yarhouse, Understanding Gender Dysphoria, p. 52.

[61] Rick Thomas and Peter Saunders in *The New Normal*, (ed. Lisa Nolland), p. 39.

[62] Rick Thomas and Peter Saunders, in Lisa Nolland (ed.), The New Normal, p.42

[63] Ibid. p.42

[64] Ibid. p.43

[65] https://www.thesun.co.uk/news/4934306/american-man-convinced-filipino-born-wrong-body/

[66] https://quillette.com/2020/01/17/why-i-resigned-from-tavistock-trans-identified-children-need-therapy-not-just-affirmation-and-drugs/

[67] Some types of operations are reversible, though with imperfect results.

Others, for example the removal of gonads, are not reversible and are therefore permanent.

[68] Andrew Walker, *God and the Transgender Debate*, pp. 74-75.

[69] Nancy Pearcey, *Love Thy Body*, p. 200

[70] Owen Strachan, *Understanding Transgender Identities*, p. 134.

[71] Andrew Walker, *God and the Transgender Debate*, p. 44.

[72] I would concur with Yarhouse that in situations of life-threatening dysphoria where there is psychiatric warrant, there may need to be flexibility with respect to the allowance of some treatments, in particular the least invasive ones (*Understanding Transgender Identities*, pp. 111-113). Moreover, leadership should also be willing to walk with the sufferer in order to support them in their discipleship (p. 122).

Part 3

Pastoral: Understanding Christian Duty within Society

Chapter 8

The Christian Voice and Secular Democracy

To summarise the biblical principles behind what we have been discussing, first, human beings are special; we are made in the image of God. This not only gives us a unique and inherent value, it also gives us the responsibility of being morally free beings. Secondly, our world is not as it was originally designed to be. It is fallen and we as humanity share that fallenness. Thirdly, God wishes our redemption, which is partly realised now, but will be fully realised in the new creation that God has prepared for us. In the meantime, He has given us objective moral standards that enable us both to live with dignity and to live successfully in community. We are on show to a broken world and giving a sense of what could and should be. Finally, the cultural trends in society and the ethical positions espoused by many are very far removed from the objective standards that God has given us.

What is our response, as people who claim a Judaeo-Christian worldview, to a culture that rejects the values of this worldview? Unfortunately, the church has not always responded appropriately, but not necessarily because of a lack of desire, spirituality or sincerity. Rather, it is because some committed and sincere Christians have failed to grasp what their role is as the church.

When the Church Fails

Some Christians have taken what could be termed a 'gospel only' approach. That is, they rightly believe in personal conversion and the need to proclaim the gospel of God's salvation through Jesus Christ, but they forget the ethical implications of the Christian life and the need to be 'salt and light'. They fearlessly proclaim salvation through Jesus, but simply expect individuals to become Christians and follow Christ, rather than realising and accepting that the Bible has much to say about culture and human flourishing.

Other Christians develop what I would term a 'monastic' approach to society. They are aware of how fallen our culture is, and so they retreat into their spiritual shells. They hide behind their church walls and sincerely worship God from inside their church buildings, but do not think that it is the business of the church to say anything about the world they live in. Some think this is the only way they can keep themselves pure. Others would rather not have to deal with the complexity of a messy world. Some might retreat because they are afraid.

Still other Christians take what can be called the 'chameleon' approach. Growing up in Africa, I often kept chameleons as pets. As a child I was intrigued to take a normally green chameleon, put it in some purple undergrowth and see it change colour to blend in. Some Christians see the vast gap between biblical standards and the wider culture. They realise how difficult it is for unchurched people to embrace the Christian faith with all its ethical requirements, and so they revise heavily what they know to be biblical truth so that they can make the Christian faith fit into culture more easily. Their rationale is that, in the same way that a chameleon adapts, so they will blend into contemporary culture and not stand out. They may think that by changing the message of the Bible, or even just downplaying it, they can make it more attractive, so as to draw more people into the church.

The problem with each of these approaches is clear. So called 'gospel only' Christians are quite correct in believing that the gospel has transformative power. However, they ignore the fact that God loves society and cares about people's lives and wants to see change in society. The 'monastic' Christians are understandably horrified by the fallenness of culture but hide away, pretending that the problems will just disappear (which of course will not happen), and in the process achieve little. The 'chameleon' Christians compromise the truth. They pander to fallen culture, perhaps out of sincere motives, but in so doing distort the clear teaching of Scripture. Moreover, they ignore its transforming power. They are like a doctor who has the medicine to heal but would rather tell the patient who is suffering that there is nothing wrong with them.

Charting a Way Forward

In contrast to these inadequate responses, the Christian responsibility within society is not to remain silent and ignore all that is going on. We are not called to create a Christian ghetto, providing safety for the chosen few and ignoring the plight of the rest. Rather, our calling is to engage with society and to share the good news. The heart of the good news is that Jesus died to save the world from sin (John 3:16). All evangelical Christians should be convinced of that and be willing to proclaim that message. But our calling as church is also to brings God's light to all of society, to model the values of the Kingdom of God and to proclaim them.

We need to be clear that this is a thoroughly biblical calling and that it has been part of the mission of both the Old Testament people of God and the New Testament people of God. In Jeremiah 29:7 God spoke to His people through His prophet commanding them 'to seek the peace and prosperity of the city'. In other words, God was concerned about the society in which Jeremiah lived and wanted His people to live in such a way as to benefit society as a whole. The church needs to face up to this challenge. If we believe God loves our community, we must be willing to serve it. Clearly that involves acts of kindness and love, but equally it involves helping people within our society to discover a better way of living. If we truly believe that God's ways are best, if we truly believe that the Maker knows what makes life flourish, then we should share that with our society.

Jesus also talked about Christians being 'salt' and 'light' (Matt. 5:13-16). Before we consider the meaning of these metaphors, we need to note that Jesus stated that we, as Christians, are both salt and light. This is not some optional extra but rather, something innate to our Christian identity. The Christian life is an active one by its very nature. Christians are meant to impact their environment and make a positive contribution to society by making it a better place.

To understand the force of Jesus' words we need to grasp what the purpose of salt was in the ancient world. First, with the lack of refrigeration it was used as a preservative. It was rubbed into meat to hold off the process of rotting. Secondly, it added savour to food, making it taste better. What Jesus was saying was that a true disciple will serve as both in society. Our society is rotting! The declining morality and rejection of Judaeo-Christian ethics require us to act so as to halt the decline. But we also want to make the world a better place, to make people's lives more palatable. We do so by telling a better story, by speaking good into culture and in so doing contribute positively to human flourishing.

Jesus also raised an important question. He asked what would happen if salt lost its salinity. Of course, sodium chloride does not change, but that culture used coarse rock salt from the Dead Sea where, at times, the sodium chloride could be washed out, leaving only grit that would then be used to cover pathways. His point was that Christians cease to be of benefit to their society if they lose their distinctive Christian voice. How can we influence society for the good if we are indistinguishable from it?

Jesus also said that we are the light of the world (v.14). In John 8:12 He refers to Himself as the light of the world. As His followers, we are to emulate Him. Light illuminates the way in the dark so that people can see where they are going. It also exposes darkness. Disciples are to expose the darkness in people's behaviour, in government and in wider culture. They are to show people how they can best live their lives and experience human flourishing. They ought to be an example to people as to how they should navigate the challenges of life.

Jesus ended this teaching section by stating that a city on a hill cannot be hidden. Anyone approaching an urban area during night time knows this. Looking at a night time aerial scene on Google Earth illustrates the point powerfully: densely populated areas really shine out. The implication is that the Christian faith should be very clearly visible. We must not hide what we believe; this must be seen and heard (v. 15). In short, our calling is to let our beliefs and worldview shine out in this dark world (v. 16) so that people can see the value of our Christian beliefs and be thankful that we are a force for good in society.

Maintaining the Balance

This is, of course, easier said than done. It becomes more complex because people who hold to conservative moral values are dismissed and ridiculed as bigots and accused of intolerance. At the same time our liberal culture, which prides itself on its own claim of being tolerant, is profoundly intolerant and condemning, especially of those who stand by their religious moral convictions.

Jesus was familiar with rejection. He urged His disciples to be as gentle as doves while at the same time being as wise as serpents (Matt. 10:16). We are to be inoffensive in society, even to the point of turning the other cheek (Matt. 5:39). But we also have to be wise, to observe what is going on in our culture. We need to note the lies, manipulations, power plays, fake news, spin, sycophancy, politicking, political correctness and dishonesty, and we need to learn how to speak truth into this complex and corrupt cultural milieu. As we do so there are two guiding principles that we must observe.

Love your Neighbour

The first of these is to love our neighbour. This is a given, but love needs properly to be understood. Loving someone means being committed to their wellbeing. Not everyone is committed to their own wellbeing, as many a drug addict or alcoholic will testify, and sometimes our love will need to be tough love. To give a simple illustration, if someone is morbidly obese, suffering from indigestion and heartburn and rapidly developing diabetes, it might seem to be an act of love to offer them another slice of cake because they say they are hungry and would like some more. This would not be a loving act. Refusing to give them another slice and thus depriving them of something they want would be an act of love, even if it might provoke their anger.

Loving one's neighbour involves proper analysis. It means asking the difficult questions and seeing the big picture. Moreover, it requires honesty and not settling for easy, superficial answers. Loving is costly; it can lead to unpopularity and criticism, but it is this kind of love that Christians need to commit to.

Prophetic Truth

Secondly, we need to speak prophetic truth into society. The Old Testament is replete with stories of prophets who brought God's message. Many of them spoke about the moral degradation of their culture and pleaded with the people to return to God and experience a change of life. They spoke out about injustice, greed and avarice as well as the demeaning of family life, sexual immorality and the oppression of the poor and the vulnerable.

The church today has that same role. While it is true that we no longer live in a Christian culture and that most people do not subscribe to a Judaeo-Christian worldview, God's values are unchanged and are the best for society. We need to make a stand and speak out against wrong and defend justice.

These two roles are not contradictory or in opposition to each other. They work together and make it possible for the church to have the maximal impact on society. As church, we care for society and love people within our community. As an act of love, we also stand up for what is right and speak out for values that will be a blessing to society. Proverbs 14:34 tells us that 'righteousness exalts a nation'. The impact of Christian influence on culture can bring great blessing to all.

Living in a Democracy

We live in a largely free democratic society. We have neither the right, nor the ability, to compel people to conform to our standards. It may be better for the institutional church to have influence rather than power. One of the lessons of the Middle Ages is that when the established church wielded temporal power, the result was corruption.

On the other hand, if Christians seek to have influence within democratic society, they are required to argue their case. They make an impact by winning the argument and persuading people within our society that biblical values are beneficial for all. Judaeo-Christian ethics should be proposed as a credible alternative to the existing moral framework. Christians should engage in the public square, not to uphold the minority rights of the Christian community alone, but for the benefit of society as a whole. Our motives are not that we want a privileged position for Christians, but that we want life to be better for all.

We Have Rights Too

Some Christians have been so reticent about arguing their case that they are not even willing to stand up for their own rights. They behave as if everyone else in society should have an opinion except Christians themselves, and they may behave this way under a guise of piety. This is not only a misunderstanding of the role of Christians in society, it is also to misunderstand how democracy works. It is also a rejection of democratic freedom for, as Roger Trigg states, 'Citizens cannot be truly free if they are not able to live according to their beliefs of what is most important'.[73] Christians who do not stand up for their own rights are not only ignoring their role as Christians, but they are also not doing justice to the freedoms of our democratic society.

In a free society Christians share the same rights as everyone else. Our voice is as valid, our opinions as deserving, as those of any other group within society. We should note too that the Apostle Paul, even though he did not live in a free democratic society, was still willing to assert his rights when the situation merited it.[74] When dealing with the Romans he did not hesitate to claim his rights of Roman citizenship (Acts 22:22-29) and when dealing with Jews he was not slow in emphasising his Jewish credentials, his connections to Judaism (Acts 22:1) or his education at the feet of an elite rabbi (Acts 22:3). Freedom of conscience and freedom of speech are two values that our society still generally embraces, and we should use them to full effect. This is being 'as wise as serpents' as Jesus advised (Matt. 10:16).

Notes

[73] Roger Trigg, *Magna Carta Unravelled*, p. 82.

[74] Kevin DeYoung, *Is it Wrong for Christians to Defend their Rights?* p. 5.

Chapter 9

Church – A Refuge for the Broken

The church welcomes all. It is a loving community that cares for the poor and the marginalised, stands up for people who cannot stand up for themselves and offers the love and embrace of family to people of all ages, backgrounds, ethnicities, social standing and orientations.

Many in our culture would say that the church is a place of intolerance, a judgmental community that cares for no one other than its own members. As Christians we suffer a great deal of negative press and are ridiculed in the public square and even by some in the great institutions in our country.

Of course, no Christian is perfect and the church is a gathering of imperfect people. Neither do Christians claim infallibility. They make mistakes. They do things they regret and recognise are wrong. Christianity should not be judged on the basis of fallible Christians, but on the perfect life and teachings of Jesus. However, many in our society do not have a fair perspective on the church and the positive contribution that Christians make to public life. They are too easily dismissed as being exclusive and prejudiced.

Christians continue to have a positive influence on society. The inspiration is Jesus Himself, who has given Christians a template for living. Jesus teaches His followers to love their enemies, to do good to those who hate them, to bless those who curse them and to pray for those who mistreat them (Luke 6:27-29). No Christian and no church does this perfectly, but it is the standard of life that Jesus requires of disciples.

Across the UK, Christians are showing love to their communities. They are supporting foodbanks, running youth clubs and children's clubs, caring for the elderly and the vulnerable in their communities and being a positive influence on society. This is despite the fact that many people do not appreciate what the church stands for.

When Christians make a stand on an ethical issue, they are often called intolerant and bigoted. However, their actions demonstrate that the Christian church cares for society and is characterised by compassion. The prophetic voice is also an example of loving others. It is because Christians believe that biblical values are good for society that we contend for them. It is not hard to see the damage that the liberal agenda has caused. We have frightening numbers of dysfunctional families and marital breakdown. Significant numbers of children grow up in single-parent families. Our personal neuroses and anxieties will not go away and neither will the use of recreational drugs and the misuse of alcohol. Our society, despite having greater wealth, opportunity and privilege than ever before, is not happier. We have sown seeds of liberalism and permissiveness hoping to be free and happy, but we have reaped a harvest of misery.

Church is a Welcoming Place

In all the changes that have occurred, the church remains a place of welcome, and Christians care about the brokenness of society and its victims, following a master who sacrificed Himself for the redemption of the world.

Church ought to be a place where people who are same-sex attracted are loved and welcomed. It should be a place of refuge for women who, in their moments of desperation and fear, have taken the lives of their unborn children. It should be a place where people suffering from gender dysphoria are welcome and will find compassion and understanding. Any church that follows the life and teachings of Jesus Christ will welcome all of these people and will not condemn, because Jesus Himself did not come to condemn the world but to save it (John 3:17).

Love requires more than just empathy. The church offers more than just compassion and welcome, it offers to help individuals get a fresh start and work towards transformation. This is not because Christians see themselves as better than anyone else. Rather, we see ourselves and everyone else as faulty and we look to our Maker for help to become what we are intended to be. Christian ethics is not just a set of propositional statements, but a pathway to healing and wholeness.

For those who Do Not Yet Believe

Some of the people who are reading this book may not be followers of Jesus Christ. I hope that I have made a reasonable case for what I believe in. My convictions come from my Christian faith and this provides the foundation for my worldview. However, I would still be committed to the ethical principles outlined in this book even if I were not a Christian. But my Christian faith is fundamental to me and it gives my life a sense of direction and purpose. My desire is that people whom I meet, including those who disagree with me, will come to experience the same joy and purpose that I have, which comes from a living experience of God in my life.

The gospel, the good news about Jesus, is available to everyone. God does not want anyone to live estranged from Himself but rather, wants everyone to believe in Him and experience the eternal life He offers (2 Pet. 3:9). This is possible because Jesus Christ died on a cross and there He took the punishment for all our faults and sins (1 Pet. 2:24). If we trust in Him and ask for His forgiveness, we can be completely cleansed (1 John 1:9). Our consciences can experience a complete reboot and we will be guilt-free before God. It does not matter what we have done; forgiveness and new life are on offer. Once someone becomes a Christian and begins the lifelong journey of following Jesus, they experience both transformation and power (2 Cor. 5:17). It is this new life that a Christian seeks to live, in a world that is fallen and disfigured by sin.

If you do not have that personal relationship with Jesus Christ, my hope is that you will respond to God's love for you and come to trust in Him. Even in our broken world, there is always hope!

Further Reading

This book raises several issues which I have not had the space to explore in any detail. This short reading list will enable you to delve deeper into these themes.

On the issue of the existence of God
Reasonable Faith by William Lane Craig, Crossway Books, 2008

On the issue of Abortion
Pro Life Answers to Pro Choice Arguments by Randy Alcorn, Multnomah Books, 2000

On the issue of a Biblical view of Homosexuality
What Does the Bible Really Teach about Homosexuality? by Kevin DeYoung, IVP, 2015

On the issue of Gender Dysphoria
Understanding Gender Dysphoria by Mark Yarhouse, IVP, 2015

On the importance of Marriage
On Marriage by Timothy Keller and Kathy Keller, Penguin Books, 2020

On human Sexuality
Why does God Care who I Sleep With? by Sam Allberry, The Good Book Company, 2020

On Same-Sex Parenting
Jepthah's Children by Robert Oscar Lopez, Brittany Klein (ed), Wilberforce Publications, London, 2016
Same-Sex Parenting Research by Walter R. Schumm, Wilberforce Publications, London, 2018

About the Author

Stephen McQuoid grew up in Ethiopia, where his parents were missionaries. He then lived in Ireland where he qualified as a nurse before going on to study theology. He has a Dip.Th. from Belfast Bible College, a BA in Biblical Studies from Trinity College, an MA and a PhD in Theology from Trinity Theological Seminary, and an MTh from the University of Wales. He has also written more than a dozen books. Stephen is the General Director of Gospel Literature Outreach, a missionary organisation based in Europe. He has an extensive training and preaching ministry that takes him throughout the UK and abroad. Stephen is married to Debbie and they have three children.

Bibliography

Atkinson, D., Field D, (Ed.), *New Dictionary of Christian Ethics and Pastoral Theology*, IVP, Leicester, 1995

Beale, G.K., We Become *What We Worship: A Biblical Theology of Idolatry*, Apollos, Leicester, 2008

Beilby James, Eddy, Paul (Ed.), *Understanding Transgender Identities: Four Views*, Baker Academic, Grand Rapids, 2019

Burgess, Samuel, *The Moral Case for Conservatism*, Wilberforce Publications, London, 2019

Brunskell-Evans H, Moore M, *Transgender Children and Young People*, Cambridge Scholars Publishing, Newcastle, 2018

Choi, Jung Min & Murphy, John W., *The Politics and Philosophy of Political Correctness*, Westport, CT: Praeger, 1992

Cragie, P C, *The Book of Deuteronomy*, WB Eerdmans, Grand Rapids, 1979

DeYoung, Kevin, *Is It Wrong for Christians to Defend their Rights?* Christian Concern Legal Centre, London, 2018

DeYoung, Kevin, *What Does the Bible Really Teach about Homosexuality?* IVP, Leicester, 2015

Feinberg John, Feinberg Paul, *Ethics for a Brave New World*, Crossway, Wheaton, 2010

Grudem, Wayne, *Christian Ethics: An Introduction to Biblical Moral Reasoning,* Crossway, Wheaton, 2018

Grudem, Wayne, *Systematic Theology*, IVP, Leicester, 2000

Johnson, A.M., Wellings, K., *Sexual Attitudes and Lifestyles*, Blackwell, Oxford, 1994

Murray, Douglas, *The Madness of Crowds*, Bloomsbury, London, 2019

Nazir-Ali, Michael, *Faith, Freedom and the Future*, Wilberforce Publications, London, 2016

Nolland, Lisa, Moseley, Carys, (Ed.) *The New Normal*, Wilberforce Publications, London, 2018

Pearse, Meic, *Why the Rest Hates the West*, SPCK, London, 2003

Pearcey, Nancy, *Love Thy Body*, Baker Books, Grand Rapids, 2018

Rose, Lynda (Ed.) *What are They Teaching the Children?* Wilberforce Publications, London, 2016

Satinover, Jeffrey, *Homosexuality and the Politics of Truth*, Baker Books, Grand Rapids, 1996

Schumm, Walter, *Same Sex Parenting Research*, Wilberforce Publications, London, 2018

Scriven, John, *Belief and the Nation*, Wilberforce Publications, London, 2013

Scriven, John (Ed.), *Magna Carta Unravelled*, Wilberforce Publications, London, 2015

Shaw, Ed, *The Plausibility Problem: The Church and Same Sex Attraction*, IVP, Leicester 2015

Walker, Andrew T., *God and the Transgender Debate*, The Good Book Company, London, 2017

Wenham, Gordon J, *Genesis 1-15* WBC, Waco, 1991

Yarhouse, Mark, Understanding Gender Dysphoria, IVP, Leicester, 2015

Zuck, Roy B (Ed.), *Vital Contemporary Issues*, Kregel, Grand Rapids, 1994

Printed in Great Britain
by Amazon

50344371R10072